POWER
SMOOTHIES

POWER
SMOOTHIES

All-Natural Fruit and Green Smoothies to Fuel Workouts, Build Muscle and Burn Fat

KEITH SEBASTIAN and **SAMUEL BARNES**

Foreword by **KRISTINE MILES**,
author of *The Green Smoothie Bible*

Ulysses Press

Published in the U.S. by
ULYSSES PRESS
P.O. Box 3440
Berkeley, CA 94703
www.ulyssespress.com

ISBN: 978-1-61243-411-7
Library of Congress Control Number 2014943037

Printed in Canada by Marquis Book Printing
10 9 8 7 6 5 4 3 2 1

Acquisitions Editor: Keith Riegert
Managing Editor: Claire Chun
Project Editor: Alice Riegert
Consulting Editor: Matt Kadey
Editor: Renee Rutledge
Proofreader: Lauren Harrison
Indexer: Sayre Van Young
Layout: Lindsay Tamura
Front cover and interior design: what!design @ whatweb.com
Cover artwork: man © Ahturner/shutterstock.com; woman © Ahturner/
    shutterstock.com; smoothies © Liv friis-larsen/shutterstock.com

Distributed by Publishers Group West

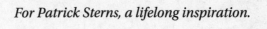

For Patrick Sterns, a lifelong inspiration.

CONTENTS

FOREWORD

My inspiration to drink green smoothies came from reading *Green for Life* by Victoria Boutenko in 2007. My passion for the humble green drink and knowledge of the human body resulted in the writing of my first book, *The Green Smoothie Bible*, which was published in 2012. The reason I love green smoothies and continue to drink them for breakfast is that they see me through all the way to lunchtime, and they are just so convenient to make and transport. My smoothie combinations provide me with fiber, fruit-based carbohydrates, good fats, plant-based proteins, vitamins, minerals and antioxidants—consumption of which results in stable blood sugar and satiation.

As a physical therapist I see athletic injuries of all ages on a daily basis, and in addition to my treatments, I also make nutritional recommendations that include adequate hydration and staying away from processed foods. I also advise seeking out protein sources as close to their natural state as possible, such as organic dairy products, legumes, nuts, seeds and leafy greens, all of which are easy to digest and are perfect for soft tissue healing and performance.

Power Smoothies is a resource I highly recommend for athletes of any age or ability who wish to complement their workouts with a nutritional guidebook that is focused on the use of whole foods and high-quality protein powders, instead of synthetic supplements and meat-based proteins. The recipes are useful and beneficial because they provide calorie- and macronutrient-data for fat, protein and carbohydrate. I like the fact that the recipes are varied, are practical single servings and contain many interesting ingredients to tempt the palate and nourish the body.

—Kristine Miles

INTRODUCTION

Stop in at a chain smoothie bar or your local convenience store and you're bound to find ready-to-drink protein smoothies geared toward packing on muscle as quickly as possible. The only problem: Many of these calorie-packed solutions are nowhere near healthy options. Sure, they've got all the necessary calories, protein, fats and carbs to effectively put on muscle, but with heavy doses of sugars and chemicals, they tend to do as much damage as they do good. This book presents the alternative option for athletes looking to increase muscle mass, stamina and general well-being: healthy, all-natural, protein-rich smoothies that nourish your entire body, including your muscles.

The recipes in this book were constructed through years of careful experimentation and research. When the two of us started training together in 2008, we found that, although fitness nutrition was a well-trodden topic, there were very few options for athletes looking to maximize athletic performance and muscle-building while still nourishing their bodies with superfoods like kale, berries and sweet potatoes, which made up the most of our individual diets. Though neither of us was vegan, or even vegetarians for that matter, we both believed deeply in diets that minimized animal products and processed foods and maximized a range of plant-based foods, particularly the healthy greens, yellows and reds of the vegetable kingdom.

Brendan Brazier's 2007 book, *Thrive: The Vegan Nutrition Guide to Optimal Performance in Sports and Life*, and Victoria Boutenko's *Green for Life* became an integral part of our everyday diet and fitness routines. And over the last several years we began to develop an entirely new approach to muscle recovery and fitness.

For the last five years, we've lived and preached the benefits of "green smoothies"—blended superfood drinks that incorporate not only fruit but also leafy green vegetables into the mix. A homemade combination of some of the most nutritious foods on the planet, from wild blueberries and papaya to bore kale and dandelion greens, creates an energizing, rejuvenating, hunger-eliminating drink with a myriad of health benefits. Green smoothies have been linked to positive effects, including positively altering mood, energy levels, the immune system and even skin, hair and nail health. As part of a nutrient-dense diet, they can also help regulate digestion and encourage weight loss. And the potent antioxidants, vitamins and minerals in each sip have been proven to help fight diseases from osteoporosis to certain forms of cancer. Green smoothies are simply life-changing.

Our goal is to meld two distinct smoothie types—superfood green smoothies that promote better health and protein-rich smoothies that build muscle, nourish the body and fill you up, so you don't turn to quick, unhealthy recovery foods. Brought together, we believe athletes of all levels can benefit from the incredible healing properties of nature's bounty while achieving the strength and fitness goals they've set out to conquer.

SECTION I

SMOOTHIES:
THE ATHLETE'S DRINK

ONE

NOURISH THE BODY

Exercise is only part of the equation when it comes to developing a lean, muscular body. The other vital part is nutrition. Regardless of your body type, natural athletic ability or metabolism speed, pairing a strong exercise regimen with the right foods (at the right times) can have a profound effect on how you look, feel and perform. But planning out the right diet takes work, science and understanding how everything you eat transforms your body.

MACRONUTRIENTS

All the food we consume on a daily basis is made up primarily of three "macronutrients"—the building blocks of physical matter and the human body's primary sources of energy: carbohydrates, protein and fat. Each of these macronutrients fills a unique and vital role, not only in allowing your body to build muscle but in making your body function properly.

CARBOHYDRATES

Think of carbohydrates, large molecules consisting only of the elements carbon, oxygen and hydrogen, as quick, easy energy. While diet fads are constantly turning carbs into dietary villains, the fact is that your healthy, functional body needs plenty of carbohydrates just to keep moving, not to mention building and maintaining muscle.

Carbohydrates are your body's high-octane energy supply. They are the main source of fuel for hardcore activities like sprinting a mile or pedaling up a steep hill. And without an adequate supply of carbs, your body is forced to slow down and start using other less-efficient sources of fuel, such as the protein stored as muscle. Don't be afraid of carbs—they keep you going strong so you can work out harder, which ultimately leads to extra calorie burning and improved muscle gains. However, there is one major caveat in all this: all carbohydrates are *not* created equal.

SIMPLE CARBOHYDRATES

You've undoubtedly heard a lot about "simple carbs" and "complex carbs." The basic form of carbohydrates ("simple carbs") are also referred to as simple sugars or monosaccharides. These include glucose (found in plants), fructose (found in fruit, flowers and honey) and galactose (found in dairy products). Each of these monosaccharides is water soluble, easily digested and absorbed directly into the bloodstream, providing the body with energy without a lot of digestive work.

Aside from the naturally occurring monosaccharides we should eat every day, we also encounter some more notorious sweets in our diet. Probably the best known is sucrose, a disaccharide, or bonded form of glucose and fructose, better known as table sugar. And in addition to plain white (or brown) sugar, there is the much talked-about high-fructose corn syrup, an artificial sweetener that ends up in many of the processed foods in our stores. While the media has absolutely portrayed processed and artificial sweeteners as much worse for you than naturally occurring sugars in fruits and vegetables, the science is actually remarkably inconclusive. In fact, natural and artificial sweeteners have more in common than they have differences. For example, each sweetener contains about 4 kilocalories of energy per gram, and they are all fairly easily converted into energy. And regardless of what type of sweetener you're consuming, your body will convert excess amounts into dreaded lipoproteins (fat).

The biggest difference is in the amounts that we end up consuming. For example, if you prepare yourself a heaping cup of fresh, sweet strawberries, you'll end up consuming about 7 grams of sugars. Scarf down a Snickers bar from the corner store and you've consumed 28 grams of sugar (four times the amount of a small bowl of delicious strawberries). That's a lot of sugar for your body to handle and probably more than you'll be able to burn off at the gym. In addition to the sugar-per-bite ratio, fruits and vegetables also help your body do some of the harder work. Fruits and vegetables are rich in antioxidants and fiber, which slow the rate at which you digest them. As a consequence, your body has time to metabolize all the plant-based sugars, which helps keep your insulin and blood sugars in balance by preventing any spikes in blood sugar levels.

COMPLEX CARBOHYDRATES

After simple carbs, there are complex carbohydrates. Complex carbohydrates, like the starch in potatoes and oats and the "dietary fiber" in kale and strawberries, are found in excellent quantity in just about every leafy green plant and many fruits. What's interesting is that while "complex carbs" are hailed as healthy and simple carbs condemned as fattening, all carbs are actually directly related to one another in chemical composition. That's because complex carbs, or polysaccharides, are made from the same carbon-oxygen-hydrogen molecules as simple sugars. Because these polysaccharides are more complex structures, however, they are metabolized much more slowly in the digestive system, providing the body with a long, even source of energy rather than a quick blood sugar spike. In addition, some of the complex carbs found in fruits and vegetables never get absorbed by the body at all; instead they get flushed out as dietary fiber, which helps maintain a healthy digestive system as well as control cholesterol levels. As a bonus, dietary fiber also makes you feel "fuller" longer, preventing you from feeling hungry shortly after you eat—which invariably can lead to overconsuming calories.

So, what should you get out of all of this? Natural is better and don't worry about carbs, because they're absolutely necessary for a healthy body. Just make sure that you are focusing your carb intake on whole grains, fruits and vegetables, making sure you get a good balance of complex carbs and simple sugars that are derived from natural plants, not man-made products like boxed cereal, energy bars or sugary protein drinks.

PROTEINS

Whenever you work out, you're essentially traumatizing your muscles—creating small tears in the muscle fibers needed to lift that barbell or take that stride. After your workout, your body responds to the trauma by repairing and rebuilding the torn muscle fibers, resulting in thicker, stronger muscle tissue. And what does your body use to repair muscle tissue? Protein.

The human body relies on 22 individual amino acids to make up proteins, 9 of which (tryptophan, threonine, isoleucine, leucine, methionine, valine, phenylalanine, lysine and histidine) cannot be sufficiently synthesized by the body and therefore are deemed essential and must be obtained through our diet. Any food item that contains all nine essential amino acids in sufficient amounts is known as a "complete protein." Available from both animal-based and plant-based sources, these complete proteins are used by the body to repair cell structures and build and maintain muscles.

Keep in mind that not all protein sources are *complete* proteins—some do not contain enough of one or more of the nine essential amino acids. For example, individually, rice and beans are considered "incomplete proteins"; however, when paired together in one dish they form a complete protein. And when your body is consuming enough complete proteins, you have what's called a positive nitrogen balance, meaning you are retaining more nitrogen from protein than you are excreting, so your body is ready to build muscles. If you are short on total and complete protein, you can have a negative nitrogen balance, forcing your body to use some muscle protein for vital bodily functions such as making cells, rather than as catalyst for muscular growth. Without a proper protein balance, you won't achieve the optimal results from your workouts with respect to your physique. At worst, chronic protein imbalance can bring about bodily harm such as reduced immunity. This is why it's vital to consume protein in amounts that are in direct relation to the length and intensity of your workouts.

As a quick rule, the average man needs 55 grams of protein and the average woman requires approximately 45 grams of protein per day to function properly. Keep in mind that those figures dictate the amount of protein needed to support proper bodily functioning and don't necessarily represent the added protein needed to support lean body mass growth and the amino acids that can be used up as fuel during prolonged periods of endurance exercise. Depending on size and gender, athletes need to add an additional 20–35 grams of protein on days that include intense aerobic exercise and an additional 45–55 grams per day when completing intense anaerobic exercises (weight training). We'll dig deeper into the best sources of protein later on in the book.

FATS

Don't be afraid of fats! Water-insoluble and derived from fatty acids and glycerol, dietary fats are also necessary for your body's optimal functionality. Of their many functions in the human body, fats help the body absorb fat-soluble vitamins

A, D, E and K. Fats are also used by the body to regulate body temperature, make hormones and repair cell structure, especially in the dermis (skin). During workouts, fats comprise your body's second-tier energy source—they're burned during activity of low to moderate intensity (like walking) to help the body preserve carbohydrates for times when intensity increases. Fats are not converted to energy as efficiently as carbohydrates, which is why the body uses them as fuel for easier activities. (During long workouts, you may start to run out of your carbohydrate stores, making it hard to keep pace during a tough exercise. But even the leanest person will find it virtually impossible to run out of fat stores during exercise.)

OMEGA-3 AND OMEGA-6 FATTY ACIDS

The most famous "good" fats are probably omega-3 and omega-6 fatty acids. Their consumption is widely encouraged because while both are essential to a healthy working body, neither of the polyunsaturated fats are naturally produced by the human body. Omega-6 fatty acids are generally found in eggs, poultry and plant oils like corn oil and soybean oil. Omega-3 fatty acids are found in fish, especially salmon and sardines, as well as plant-based sources like flaxseed and walnuts.

While diets containing ample amounts of omega-3 and omega-6 fatty acids have been linked with healthier brain cell membranes, lower cholesterol and a reduced risk of heart disease, ongoing scientific research has edged toward omega-3 fatty acids as being the slightly healthier of the two but has shown that Americans consume too much omega-6 fatty acids and not enough omega-3s. Strive to balance your daily intake of omega-3s and omega-6s, with a target quantity for the average adult around 2 grams of omegas each day.

It's also important to know that different types of fats can be more beneficial than others. In general, fats contain fatty acid chains, chains of carbon atoms paired with a number of hydrogen atoms. Unsaturated fats (monounsaturated fats and polyunsaturated fats) contain at least one double-bonded carbon atom. Monounsaturated fats contain exactly one, while polyunsaturated fats contain more than one. Omega fatty acids, found in certain grains, nuts, seeds and fish oil, refer to unique structural formations of polyunsaturated fats.

For decades, the "bad" fats have been identified as saturated fats and trans fats—and have been blamed for epidemics of high cholesterol levels, obesity and heart disease. However, recent studies have flipped the script a bit when it comes to natural saturated fats like those found in coconut oil and animal products such as dairy. Saturated fats have every carbon atom paired with as many hydrogen atoms as possible, and the complex chains allow the fats to retain their shape and bonds longer—saturated fats don't spoil as quickly as unsaturated fats and they don't melt at room temperature—which, of course, makes them ideal ingredients for processed foods that require long shelf lives. And it's exactly their role in packaged, processed products that has given saturated fats such a bad reputation. The truth is that natural sources of saturated fats— like coconut milk and oil—can help the body perform properly when consumed in moderation.

Trans fats, on the other hand, often found in fried foods, packaged foods and greasy baked goods, are for the most part man-made fats and much worse than saturated fats. In fact, they are so bad for you that they are heavily regulated or even banned in several countries, and will likely be regulated to some extent in the U.S. before too long. They are now being removed from an increasing number of packaged foods and restaurant menus.

"Good" fats are monounsaturated fats, polyunsaturated fats and omega fatty acids. Monounsaturated fats come from "lighter," more natural plant-based foods and products. Nuts, nut butters, avocados and vegetable oils are good sources of monounsaturated fats. Fish, soy milk and flaxseed are all good sources of polyunsaturated fats. Foods high in good fats can actually help you lose weight for a number of reasons: They help you feel full more quickly, preventing you from needlessly snacking, and they appear to help with maintaining a higher metabolism.

VITAMINS, ANTIOXIDANTS AND MINERALS

Eat your fruits and veggies! In a world where the health benefits of everything you put into your body can be hotly contested, it's nice to have two food groups that have very little downside. The USDA recommends that adults consume a minimum of two servings of fruit and three servings of vegetables per day... minimum. The amount of fruit increases to three servings for athletes consuming 2,000 calories or more each day with the suggested consumption of vegetables remaining the same. Based on the last five years of experimentation, we think these quantities are too low. In order to maintain a healthy, physically strong body, you should consume a minimum of four servings of fruit and five servings of vegetables each day.

But just why are fruits and vegetables so good for an active body? It's pretty simple, actually. Fruits and vegetables are the most efficient way to obtain the vitamins, minerals, antioxidants and dietary fiber you need to function optimally. A properly balanced diet full of fruits and vegetables can bring about incredible health benefits ranging from boosting your immune system, improving digestion and lowering the risk for heart disease, certain cancers and diabetes to generally slowing the aging process.

A diet rich in fruits and vegetables is also vital for athletes. Not only are the carbohydrates found in fruits and vegetables excellent sources of fuel for any form of exercise, but the vitamins and antioxidants they contain help boost immune function, which can be negatively affected during periods of rigorous exercise. And, of course, if you're an older athlete, fruits and vegetables can keep your heart in top working condition, reducing your risk of heart disease and allowing you to continue challenging yourself athletically for years to come.

VITAMINS

Vitamins are organic compounds that the human body needs in small amounts in order to survive, yet cannot synthesize (enough of) internally to meet overall needs. Therefore, the body must turn to an external source, namely food. Different vitamins serve different functions, and vitamin deficiencies can lead to serious illnesses and poor athletic performance. The following are the essential vitamins the human body needs and what role they play in health:

VITAMIN A: Essential in maintaining healthy skin, vision, bones and immune function. Carotenoids, such as beta-carotene, in foods can be converted in the body into vitamin A.

VITAMIN B1 (THIAMINE): Plays an essential role in nerve function and releasing energy from glucose.

VITAMIN B2 (RIBOFLAVIN): Vital for vision and skin health and producing energy from protein, fat and carbs.

VITAMIN B3 (NIACIN): Aids in nerve function, digestion and maintaining healthy, beautiful skin.

VITAMIN B5 (PANTOTHENIC ACID): Helps convert fatty acids, glucose and proteins to energy; it also aids in maintaining healthy skin.

VITAMIN B6 (PYRIDOXINE): Helps convert protein, carbs and fat into energy and supports the cardiovascular system.

VITAMIN B7 (BIOTIN): Helps metabolize energy and ensure healthy skin and hair.

VITAMIN B9 (FOLIC ACID): Vital for cell division and the regeneration of blood cells, and essential during pregnancy for fetal nervous system development.

VITAMIN B12 (COBALAMIN): Helps promote nerve function and generate new cells.

VITAMIN C (ASCORBIC ACID): Crucial for immune function, iron absorption and the production of healing collagen proteins.

VITAMIN D: Helps maintain healthy bones via its role in improving calcium absorption.

VITAMIN E: Antioxidant that helps maintain cell health and aids in protection of red blood cells.

VITAMIN K: Necessary for bone health (helps prevent osteoporosis) and in regulating the blood's ability to properly clot after injury.

ANTIOXIDANTS

Oxidation is a chemical reaction in which the electron from one atom is lost to another. In nature, the oxidative process results in all sorts of chemical reactions—from the forming of rust on iron to the combustion of wood into fire. In the human body, the oxidation of electrons within molecules releases "free radicals," molecular compounds that have lost an electron and are thus capable of chemically bonding with other molecules in the body.

While these free radicals are produced naturally in the body all the time, in high concentrations they can lead to dangerous cellular damage, which can lead to premature aging on the cellular level, and have been linked to a number of chronic diseases such as cancer. In their attempt to pair with any available electron, free radical molecules can break otherwise stable bonds on the cellular level. And the damage can be to cells, enzymes, even right down to your DNA. Antioxidants, like vitamins A, C and E, as well as the numerous phytochemicals found in plant-based foods, act as microscopic missile interceptors—inhibiting your body's cellular oxidation by intercepting the free radicals and bonding with them and thereby rendering them less harmful.

Keep in mind that there's no way to escape the production of free radicals in the human body. In fact, vigorous aerobic exercise, a hallmark of a healthy body, can increase your body's oxidative stress through the simple act of breathing in more oxygen than normal. To help combat this, focus on consuming plenty of antioxidant-rich foods throughout the day, such as the fruits and vegetables listed on the following page, and blended into many of the smoothies that follow.

SLEEP: THE BEST ANTIOXIDANT

Aside from the fact that a good night's sleep is vital for proper muscle recovery, growth and general physical health, it also provides your body with one of nature's most powerful antioxidants—melatonin. Unlike antioxidants from fruits and vegetables, melatonin is produced naturally in your body as part of your circadian sleep cycle, telling your body it is time to go to sleep. But melatonin also serves another purpose in your body—it's known as a sort of "suicide antioxidant," in that it actively searches out some of the most damaging free radicals, bonds with them and then is flushed out of the body.

Over the last couple of years there has been a bit of controversy regarding the exact measuring of antioxidants. In 2012, the USDA withdrew its signature antioxidant scale—the Oxygen Radical Absorbance Capacity (ORAC) scale—because they found it impossible to prove whether the levels of antioxidants in foods they were measuring in labs were actually the same as you would find at the supermarket. For example, in the lab açaí (a fruit found in the Amazon) scored off-the-charts with a 102,700 ORAC score (compared to 6,552 for blueberries), while store-bought options were found to contain significantly lower scores.

HIGH-ANTIOXIDANT SMOOTHIE-FRIENDLY INGREDIENTS

Fruits

Açaí

Avocados

Blackberries

Blueberries

Chokeberries

Cranberries

Currants

Elderberries

Goji Berries

Plums

Raspberries

Red Delicious Apples

Veggies

Arugula

Beet Greens

Kale

Red-Leaf Lettuce

Spinach

Grains

Oats

Sweet Additions

Dark Chocolate

Cinnamon

Molasses

Pure Maple Syrup

Nuts/Seeds

Almonds

Chia Seeds

Flaxseeds

Hazelnuts

Pecans

Pistachios

Walnuts

Legumes

Black Beans

Kidney Beans

Lentils

Peanuts (and Peanut Butter)

Pinto Beans

Soybeans

What we do know, however, is that there are plenty of fruits and vegetables that contain enormous amounts of antioxidants, and regardless of their scores, they are very good for you! Like general nutritional content, antioxidants degrade over time, so it's best to find fruits and vegetables that are at their freshest— including locally sourced produce or flash-frozen options that lock in the nutrition.

MINERALS

Dietary minerals are chemical compounds that, like vitamins, the human body needs but cannot produce sufficiently on its own. The following are the dietary minerals most beneficial to the human body's ability to survive and thrive, along with their unique role in promoting health:

CALCIUM: Needed for healthy bone growth, muscle contraction, nerve signal transmission and blood clotting.

CHOLINE: Helps produce brain neurotransmitters and cells.

CHROMIUM: Essential for proper blood sugar levels.

COPPER: Helps the body metabolize iron and produce melanin (tan) to protect the skin from sunburns.

FLUORIDE: Important for bone growth and prevention of cavities in the teeth.

IODINE: Helps in thyroid hormone production.

IRON: Necessary for healthy red blood cells and some enzymes.

MAGNESIUM: Helps regulate the rhythm of the heart, muscle and nerve function, and aids in bone strength.

MANGANESE: Helps form bones.

MOLYBDENUM: Helps the body form certain enzymes.

PHOSPHORUS: Helps bones grow; helps with energy levels; necessary for proper cell functionality.

POTASSIUM: An electrolyte necessary for proper fluid balance; controls blood pressure.

SELENIUM: Necessary for the regulation of thyroid hormones and cell protection; acts as an antioxidant.

SODIUM: One of the most necessary (and potentially dangerous) minerals in our diet is sodium. First, the positives. Sodium is vital to your survival. At the optimal amounts, sodium helps regulate blood pressure and blood volume by maintaining the correct fluid balance throughout your body, and it helps promote normal muscle and nerve function. But *too much* sodium can be really dangerous for some people, especially people who are sodium-sensitive and have trouble eliminating excess sodium through urine. For these people, sodium buildup over time can cause a chain reaction of dangerous consequences: First, your blood volume increases, which forces your heart to pump harder, creating an increase in blood pressure. Over time, this can lead to heart disease, liver disease, stroke and heart failure. Everybody should limit their sodium intake to less than 2,300 milligrams per day (about 1 teaspoon of table salt); however, people with any of the above symptoms should keep their sodium intake under 1,500 grams per day.

Avoid frozen foods and prepared foods, including breads and prepackaged meals.

ZINC: Aids in immune functions and nerve function. Zinc also helps make testosterone, one of the body's primary muscle-building hormones.

While it's possible to obtain some of your dietary minerals through multivitamins and other sources, plant foods are some of the most efficient and direct sources of minerals, as plants can absorb minerals via the soil they grown in.

GET YOUR SUPERFOOD FIX!

Superfoods are fruits, vegetables and other food sources that are unusually high in antioxidants, vitamins and dietary minerals. Examples of superfoods are berries like blueberries, nuts like almonds, dark green vegetables like kale, brightly colored vegetables like beets or sweet potatoes, citrus fruits like tangerines, certain fatty fish like salmon or sardines, and legumes like lentils or peanuts (and chocolate!). Exercise combined with a healthy, superfood-rich diet can ensure a healthy body, improve energy levels and increase your longevity.

TWO

WHAT GOES INTO YOUR SMOOTHIE

Now that you've gotten a pretty good idea of what your body needs to thrive, let's talk about a key way of getting there—smoothies! What are they? Why do we love them? How do we make them? The smoothies you're going to find in this book are composed of four basic ingredients: fruit, vegetables, protein and a liquid base. Throw those four elements into a blender and you end up with a drink that offers a nearly complete nutritional package, vital energy, dietary fiber and up to half of your daily protein needs. And when you're in the middle of athletic training, this type of food/energy/protein delivery system is a vital way of achieving your fitness goals.

Not everyone wants to lug a peanut butter and jelly sandwich or energy bar to the gym every day to make sure they're getting the recovery food they need after a tough workout.

Furthermore, not everyone wants to *eat* a sandwich or energy bar every day after the gym. Smoothies offer a quick, easy and, best of all, palatable way of getting the healthy stuff you need. But in addition to the efficiency of smoothies in delivering macronutrients, vitamins, minerals and antioxidants with minimal work, blending your greens and fruit has a number of other incredible benefits.

THE GREAT FIBER CONTROVERSY

Let's get this out there right now: Juicing and blending are not the same thing! So, let's dispel the nasty little rumor that has moved from juicing to smoothies: Blending your fruit and greens will not destroy the fiber! You've probably heard about this controversy regarding the "juice fasting" craze—juicing fruits and vegetables removes dietary fiber from your diet and leaves you with a drink, depending on what it is you are juicing, with a high concentration of sugar. Well, while that may be true about juicing, it's not true when it comes to blending. And the reasons are fairly self-evident—the blades of a blender do no more damage to fibrous fruits and vegetables than your teeth are capable of inflicting. Furthermore, consider that the fiber you ingest from a piece of fruit or leafy green vegetable is able to survive a trip through your mouth, stomach juices and rough-and-tumble digestive tract completely intact. Dietary fiber is incredibly resilient, and a minute or two even in the best blender is not going to remove its healthy goodness. With that in mind, let's get blending!

LET THERE BE CHLOROPHYLL!

Adding leafy green vegetables to your smoothies is a fantastic way of increasing the nutrient-, vitamin-, antioxidant- and fiber-content of your smoothies. But they also add one of nature's most incredible creations—chlorophyll. Head out into a garden, field or forest and you'll see chlorophyll all around you; it's the biomolecule that gives plants their green color. In nature, chlorophyll is a vital part of photosynthesis, the process that converts light energy from the sun into the plant energy that allows for growth. In blending your greens, you release that chlorophyll into a rich liquid that makes drinking a tall glass of blended greens a bit like consuming the life-giving power of the sun!

Interestingly, the molecular makeup of chlorophyll (a magnesium ion bonded in a nitrogen casing with a hydrocarbon tail) is also very similar in composition to a life-supporting element pumping through all of our bodies—heme. Heme is a primary component of hemoglobin, the metalloprotein found in all human blood that is responsible for transporting oxygen around the body and gives blood its red color.

What does that mean? Well, the science is undecided on whether raw chlorophyll can boost our health (and in all honesty, there have been plenty of snake-oil products proclaiming chlorophyll an age-reversing cure-all), but many proponents of green smoothies equate, however unappealingly, that drinking blended chlorophyll is akin to receiving an infusion of fresh blood right into your digestive tract. It's a bit of a gross concept, but the idea is nice. The real health benefits are probably somewhere in between the two extremes. Regardless, the biomolecule that powers 98 percent of life on earth is worth savoring every day, whether in your garden or in your glass.

UNLEASH YOUR NUTRIENTS

In addition to releasing copious amounts of chlorophyll, the blending process allows for the easier digestion of nutrients. The unfortunate fact is that human bodies do not make for the best vegetarians. Everything from the shape of our teeth to our complicated digestive systems has been adapted for an omnivore's diet. We're designed to tear meat, grind nuts and chew up greens. What we're not naturally capable of doing is getting the most out of everything we eat. Compare our digestive process to that of a grazing cow (which has a stomach with four individual compartments) and it's pretty clear that we don't fare particularly well subsisting on plants alone. In this regard, blending is a wonderful technological adaptation that allows us to get more out of our fruits and greens. By putting those ingredients in the blender, you are essentially pre-digesting your reds, yellows and greens—kind of like taking the time to really, *really* chew your food. We can all admit that eating slowly might not be our forte in life.

CHOOSING A BLENDER

Many smoothie fanatics can have pretty strong opinions when it comes to choosing a blender. Talking to someone who blends religiously can be a little like talking to an automobile enthusiast who knows every detail of this year's supercars. What's the RPM of your blender motor? Polycarbonate container or glass? NSF certified? It can be a little daunting. And blenders come in every imaginable price range from ultra-cheap to uber-expensive.

High-end blenders like those by Blendtec, Ninja or Vitamix offer a couple of major pluses: For one, the smoothie consistency (texture and taste) is far greater than a low- or mid-range blender option offers. The other benefit of high-end blenders is that they wear out much slower than lower-priced blenders. This may not sound like the biggest selling point, but if you become a hardcore smoothie drinker you will *destroy* blenders—even those in the $200–$300 range. Typically, our experience is that a daily smoothie drinker will completely wear out a mid-range blender in one-and-a-half to two years. High-end blenders, on the other hand, come with three-year warranties and, barring any defects, will last you a lot longer than that.

So what should you do? Well, we believe in keeping this a completely personal choice. Don't feel like you have to spring for a $700 Vitamix off the bat; your everyday blender will do just fine. Start wherever you're comfortable, but make sure you do your research. You want to buy a blender that's going to last at least your first year of blending while keeping you healthy and safe. Blenders can be nasty harbingers of bacteria if they're not cleaned often and properly, so make sure you're purchasing something that's not going to be too difficult to clean *daily*. Otherwise, you can run the risk of bacterial poisoning (including salmonella and E. coli) or worse. Also, make sure the container (including the blades) have been approved by the NSF, a third-party public health and safety organization that monitors the chemical composition of consumer products. The main concern with blenders is avoiding having the plastic chemicals from cheap containers leach into your smoothies. If you get into the smoothie lifestyle (and have the available funds), we absolutely suggest upgrading to a Vitamix or Blendtec. They really do make a difference in your smoothie experience over the long run.

CHOOSING ORGANIC VS. CONVENTIONAL

What you put into your smoothies has a big effect on your body. Choosing fresh, ripe ingredients can make all the difference in how many nutrients your body absorbs. But how clean your ingredients are matters just as much. The Environmental Working Group releases an annual list of the produce they consider to be the "Dirty Dozen"—fruits and vegetables that have been tested and determined to have the highest concentration of pesticides and other chemicals due to conventional industrialized farming practices. Because pesticides and chemicals can be absorbed into your body right from the foods you eat, and because those chemicals can be extremely harmful to your body, hormone balance and immune system, it is highly recommended that you buy organic selections of these fruits and vegetables. The list changes every year, though some produce are common repeat offenders. For 2014, the Dirty Dozen was:

- Apples*
- Strawberries*
- Grapes*
- Celery*

- Peaches*
- Spinach*
- Sweet Bell Peppers
- Nectarines*

- Cucumbers*
- Potatoes
- Cherry Tomatoes
- Hot Peppers
- Kale*

indicates a common smoothie or green smoothie ingredient

It's important to note that while not on the top 13 list, many staple ingredients of smoothies, like blueberries, blackberries, raspberries and collards, were also found to have high pesticide contamination levels and should always be purchased organic.

Of course, purchasing all organic produce has its own drawbacks, primarily because organic fruits and vegetables can be prohibitively expensive. So, make sure you're spending your money wisely. Not all fruits and vegetables absorb pesticides and chemicals the same way; some require less chemical treatment while others have natural barriers, like thick skins, that block exposure. If you don't have the means to buy *all* organic, the 2014 "Clean 15" fruits and vegetables that follow can be purchased in their "conventional" or "non-organic" form.

- Avocados*
- Sweet Corn
- Pineapple*
- Cabbage
- Sweet Peas
- Onions
- Asparagus
- Mangoes*
- Papayas*
- Kiwis*
- Eggplants
- Grapefruit*
- Cantaloupe*
- Cauliflower
- Sweet Potatoes*

indicates a common smoothie or green smoothie ingredient

Of course, you should update your list annually as cultivation practices may change. The website is www.ewg.org.

GROWING YOUR OWN FRUITS AND VEGETABLES

Another way to ensure the health of your fruits and vegetables is to grow what you can on your own. And when it comes to fruits, vegetables and herbs, the fresher the better. And while most people would agree that fresher fruits and vegetables taste better, they might not know that many plant foods also begin to degrade nutritionally the moment they're picked. Fruits and vegetables can take upward of an entire month to get from the tree to the table, especially foods grown in the Southern Hemisphere. When you factor in transportation, time spent on the shelves and time spent in the fridge, even foods grown within the U.S. can sit for up to *two weeks* before they're consumed. Growing your own edible garden is not only fun and economical, but will enable you to get more nutrition from every leaf, sprig and fruit you consume.

A lot of people are afraid of growing their own fruits and vegetables. They think it takes a green thumb and a lot of patience to grow a verdant edible garden. But while some edible garden foods do require a ton of TLC, many delicious, healthy green smoothie ingredients are surprisingly easy to grow. Even if you think you don't have the magical homesteading touch, give it a try; with the proper blend of soil, moisture and sunshine, even the least experienced gardeners can have a rich home garden in weeks! Here's a crash course in growing your own veggie garden.

CHOOSING A SPACE: Your first job is to choose a space for your edible garden. If you live in a small, urban apartment, chances are you only have enough room for a single small planter box. If you have a big yard, you'll need to decide between planting in rows and building backyard planter boxes. While row planting is cheaper and easier, it requires more expertise and attention. If you're just starting out, we suggest beginning with raised planter boxes, which provide deeper soil reserves for healthy root growth.

SUNSHINE: Most plant foods require at least a little bit of direct sunshine. If you have the option, choose the brightest, sunniest spots for your planter boxes. If you don't have a super-sunny spot, don't panic; many vegetables such as arugula, spinach and certain lettuces do fine in partially shaded areas.

SOIL: Having the right kind of soil is crucial if you want to grow a lush, healthy garden. Planting soil or compost is available at most nurseries, and both usually have the right balance of nutrients to help jump-start your veggies. More advanced homesteaders may want to amend their current soil with homegrown compost or other organic matter. Whichever avenue you choose, make sure your soil is organic, rich and devoid of rocks or "cakey" clumps. Also, it should drain relatively easily—but not too quickly.

WATER: If your veggie garden isn't getting enough water by rain or moisture, you will need to water by hand or set up an irrigation system. Your veggies will tell you when they aren't getting enough water by wilting. Soil is another good indicator of your plant's water needs. If you have proper soil, you can simply check to see if it's dry or moist and add water accordingly.

WHAT TO GROW?

SINGLE SMALL BOX: If you only have one small planter box, you'll want to maximize your yields by choosing fast-growing foods that produce a high a percentage of edible material. Herbs like cilantro, mint, basil, parsley and rosemary all do great in small areas. Veggies such as arugula, spinach and lettuce can also thrive in tightly packed spaces. If your planter box is deep and receives a steady stream of sunshine, you may even have success with tomatoes in the summer months.

LARGER BACKYARD GARDENS: If you have more space, we recommend utilizing it! And for long-term gains, we suggest planting fruit trees and bushes. Fruit tends to be the most expensive produce to purchase, especially if you are buying fresh, organic options, so if you have the opportunity to grow it yourself, you should. Apple, plum, fig and even avocado trees can grow well throughout the United States with a few exceptions in colder climates. Before you plant any seeds, however, do your research to find out what varietal grows best in your specific location. For example Akane apples are best suited to growing in warm climates like Southern California, whereas Ruby Frost apples thrive in northern cold climates. There are thousands of options available. Citrus trees, especially lemon, grow easily, and some breeds have been cultivated to take up minimal space. Other fruits like strawberries, raspberries and even blackberries can grow great in planter boxes or in small greenhouses, and there's nothing better than growing your own superfoods! Berry plants will yield fruit in late May through early October, and you can always freeze the extra fruit to hold you through the rest of the year. Tomatoes are an especially popular home garden vegetable, as they are easy to grow and produce loads of fresh, ripe fruit.

You can fill out the rest of your planter boxes with a variety of veggies and herbs, depending on the season, climate and sunshine levels. Leafy green vegetables such as arugula, spinach and lettuces grow well in shadier parts of your backyard and will survive winters in areas of the country that don't receive too many days of hard frost. Kale, on the other hand, is at its best from September to January and actually gets more delicious and nutritious as the temperature drops. Dandelion greens (often considered just another nuisance weed) are great from March to June. Certain herbs like mint and basil grow best during the hotter summer months, but other herbs like rosemary can thrive all year round. Experiment with your garden and see what grows best. If you're having trouble getting started or knowing how much space to leave between plants, or just want advice about what fruits and veggies will grow well in your garden, don't be afraid to ask at your local nursery. But most of all, have fun with your home garden.

FRESH OR FROZEN?

There's nothing quite like biting into a freshly picked piece of fruit, still warm from the summer sun. But let's face it, most of us don't have the opportunity to walk outside and pick our produce straight from the living, thriving plant. The unfortunate fact of store-bought produce is that as soon as the piece of fruit or bunch of greens is picked, the clock starts ticking on its nutritional deterioration. The first victims of fruit aging are normally the water-soluble vitamins, like the B vitamins and vitamin C, also a powerful antioxidant. If you're leaving your fresh fruit and vegetables out for too long, you might be losing valuable nutrients!

The solution? Refrigeration and freezing. If you have fruits or vegetables that you're just not going to be able to use quickly enough, especially those locally grown gems from the farmers' market, don't wait to throw them away. Instead, grab some Tupperware or a freezer bag and preserve them yourself. While many water-filled fruits and vegetables (like blueberries, watermelon and kale) lose their crisp texture once frozen and thawed, a smoothie made with those frozen treats eliminates any unpleasant texture problem all together. You may lose a little bit of flavor, but the nutritional content and palatable qualities of the fresh fruit will still come out in your ice-cold smoothie.

FREEZING YOUR LIQUID ASSETS

If you enjoy adding a liquid base to your smoothies that doesn't come cheap or should only be consumed in moderation (like coconut water, coconut milk or pomegranate juice) and you don't use a lot of the base in each smoothie, save your fresh liquid ingredients for later by freezing them in an ice cube tray. Then add one or two cubes each time you blend a smoothie. Freezing your liquids will prevent them from spoiling or losing most of their nutritional content, and you'll end up with exciting flavors to punch up any blend.

In addition to saving good fresh produce from going bad, purchasing pre-packaged frozen fruits and vegetables is another excellent choice, especially if you're trying to save money.

Pre-packaged frozen fruits and veggies are often frozen by the grower before they have any time to degrade while sitting on the supermarket shelf, meaning they have almost the same nutritional content as if they were being eaten right off the plant. So you're consuming produce that is most likely much fresher than the "fresh" produce available in your local supermarkets, which have likely traveled thousands of miles (and up to a week since they were first picked).

In addition to being nutritionally rich, packaged frozen produce tends to be significantly cheaper than fresh, out-of-season produce and is available all year round, allowing you to enjoy your favorite berries, greens and tropical fruits well into the cold winter months. Just remember to abide by all the same rules as you would with fresh fruit—if it's a "Dirty" item, buy organic, and always wash your frozen produce before you blend it.

SECTION II

DRINK YOUR GREENS (AND REDS AND YELLOWS...): NUTRITION FACTS

THREE

FRUITS AND NATURAL SWEETENERS

STAPLE FRUITS

These fruits are very widely available year round in the United States. Even beyond the supermarket, you can find them at delis, convenience stores and cafes, and they make great smoothie options when you're in a pinch.

APPLES

SERVING SIZE: 1 cup (125 grams)		CALORIES: 65
CARBS: 17 grams	PROTEIN: 0 grams	FAT: 0 grams

There's a reason the apple was the fruit in the Garden of Eden—these gems are among the earliest fruits to be cultivated by man, in large part because they are essentially pre-packaged bundles of energy. Apples are a great source of quick carbs and water, which makes them ideal for a pre-workout energy boost. In addition, they provide a decent source of vitamin B6, which helps the body regulate the release of glucose from glycogen, the main energy source of fast-paced exercise. Aside from their energy-providing properties, apples are also great for your overall health: They're an excellent source of dietary fiber, helping the body regulate not only blood sugar levels, but digestion as well; and their high vitamin C content helps your skin's collagen replenish itself, helping stave off wrinkles and other signs of aging. Apples also contain trace amounts of numerous other vitamins and minerals, including niacin, folate, calcium, iron, magnesium, potassium, copper, manganese and vitamin K, which has been proven to play a vital role in bone health. The fruit is also a source of the potent antioxidant quercetin. Be forewarned, however: A serving of apples contains 13 grams of sugar, so consume them in moderation.

BANANAS

SERVING SIZE: 1 cup (225 grams)		CALORIES: 200
CARBS: 51 grams	PROTEIN: 2 grams	FAT: 1 gram

With their high carbohydrate content, bananas make an ideal pre-workout snack. Not only do those carbs provide you with the energy necessary for a rigorous workout, but a serving of bananas provides 23 percent of the Recommended Daily Value (RDV) of potassium, which is vital for normal nerve and muscle function. Bananas may also prevent exercise-associated muscle cramping, as low potassium levels in the blood may contribute to muscle cramps or muscular weakness. However, a myth surrounding bananas is that they can stop a cramp if you eat one after the cramp begins. This has been proven untrue. It takes between 30 minutes and an hour and half for banana consumption to alter the potassium levels in your bloodstream, so eat your bananas *before* you exercise if you want to avoid cramping.

ORANGES

SERVING SIZE: 1 cup (170 grams)		CALORIES: 100
CARBS: 26 grams	PROTEIN: 2 grams	FAT: 1 gram

Cultivated since antiquity throughout Asia, oranges are a favorite fruit across the globe because they are sweet, juicy and provide a ton of vitamin C (a large orange can provide over 160 percent your daily value). A diet rich in vitamin C can boost the immune system. Oranges also contain moderate amounts of vitamin A, vitamin B6, vitamin B12, potassium and calcium, which is important for maintaining healthy bones. The common "orange" is technically called the "sweet orange" for a reason: A large orange contains 17 grams of sugar, so add them to your smoothies in moderation.

BERRIES

Common berries are (at least in everyday language) fruits that develop from multiple ovaries of a single flower, giving them that textured, globular appearance. Berries tend to be small, sweet and full of powerful antioxidants. Unfortunately, most berries are only in season during the late spring and summer. Frozen berries, however, are readily available and add a cold, icy crunch to any out-of-season berry smoothie.

COMMON BERRIES VS. BOTANICAL BERRIES: THE CONFUSING TRUTH

Unless you're a botanist or a fruit aficionado, you probably didn't know that the word "berry" technically refers to any fruit that grows from a solitary ovary. Under this definition, blackberries, strawberries and raspberries *are not* berries, but avocados, tomatoes, bananas, watermelons and even pumpkins *are* berries. To differentiate, the things we actually call berries are known as "common berries," while the latter are called "botanical berries."

BLACKBERRIES

SERVING SIZE: 1 cup (144 grams)		CALORIES: 62
CARBS: 15 grams	PROTEIN: 2 grams	FAT: 1 gram

A cup of blackberries contain nearly half of your daily requirement of vitamin C, as well as vitamin K and folate, a water-soluble vitamin that has been linked to decreasing the risk of strokes, having potent anti-aging properties and a causing a positive effect on depression and mood stabilization. Blackberries also contain large quantities of copper and manganese along with trace amounts of calcium, iron, magnesium, phosphorus, potassium, zinc and selenium. Because blackberries have a hefty dose of fiber, they make great additions to morning smoothies to help keep you feeling full throughout the day.

BLUEBERRIES

SERVING SIZE: 1 cup (148 grams)		CALORIES: 84
CARBS: 15 grams	PROTEIN: 1 gram	FAT: 0 grams

One of the world's great superfoods, blueberries, like blackberries, pack a lot of vitamin C in a small package. But their true strength lies in their high content of vitamin K. Like vitamin D, vitamin K has a tremendous effect on bone health, assisting with the binding of calcium to the bone structure. A cup of blueberries will also provide your body with trace quantities of iron, magnesium, phosphorus, potassium, zinc and copper, along with up to 25 percent of your daily suggested value of manganese. Blueberries also have been proven to improve cognitive function, especially in older adults, as well as improving alertness—they act as sort of natural caffeine, making them ideal for morning smoothies.

RASPBERRIES

SERVING SIZE: 1 cup (123 grams)		CALORIES: 64
CARBS: 15 grams	PROTEIN: 1 gram	FAT: 1 gram

The powerful anti-inflammatory phytonutrients within raspberries have long been hailed for their cancer-fighting abilities—they may help reduce the chances of developing colon, prostate, cervical and breast cancers. The anti-inflammatory properties of raspberries also make them an ideal addition to any smoothie after a particularly rigorous workout. The benefits of these delicious berries don't stop there; raspberries are an excellent source of dietary fiber, vitamins B6, C, E and K, as well as magnesium and manganese.

STRAWBERRIES

SERVING SIZE: 1 cup (152 grams)		CALORIES: 49
CARBS: 12 grams	PROTEIN: 1 gram	FAT: 0 grams

While strawberries contain an immense amount of vitamin C (149 percent of your daily value, to be exact), they also deliver dietary fibers, potassium, magnesium and folate. Strawberries are a common ingredient in many smoothies because of their sweet, tangy flavor and their rich, red color.

STONE FRUITS

Stone fruits, so called because of the large, rock-hard seed in the center of the fruit flesh, are delightful, juicy fruits at their peak from late spring to early fall. Their high water content, unique flavor and limited growing season make stone fruits a wonderful change-of-pace centerpiece for summertime smoothies. Some people don't like throwing stone fruits into their smoothies because they find removing the large pits a nuisance, but they are well worth the extra few minutes of added prep time.

At first glance, stone fruits may not appear as mind-blowingly nutritious as some of the more en vogue fruits out there, but they are rich in potassium and contain antioxidants such as vitamin C and carotenoids, which can help improve eyesight. Finally, recent studies show that stone fruits contain a crack team of bioactive compounds that work in conjunction to prevent metabolic syndrome, which can lead to major health problems like obesity and diabetes.

Unfortunately, stone fruits are very delicate and especially susceptible to spring and fall frosts. Because of their delicacy and short, abundant season, stone fruits are favorite canning and jamming choices—a smoothie-ingredient option that can make it possible to enjoy the sweet succulent fruits of summer well into the winter months. Stone fruits can also be frozen when in season and used for smoothies throughout the year.

CHERRIES

SERVING SIZE: 1 cup (138–155 grams)		CALORIES: 77–87
CARBS: 19–22 grams	PROTEIN: 1–2 grams	FAT: 0 grams

Sweet and sour cherries are not only delicious, bite-size treasures, but these may be nature's pain reliever and sleep aid in one delicious little package! While nothing from the nutritional profile jumps out at you—they're decent sources of vitamin C and potassium, but what fruit isn't?—they *do* have some hidden nutritional gems: The stuff that gives cherries their shiny red color—anthocyanin—may be as effective at reducing inflammation as ibuprofen, without the potentially dangerous side effects! Finally, cherries also contain more melatonin, a natural hormone that can aid in sleep, than almost any natural source. So pop some pitted cherries in the blender after a strenuous, late-night workout, and watch yourself drift off into a deep, painless sleep. Both sweet and tart cherries are high in sugar, and sweet cherries contain less of the good stuff than do sour cherries.

PEACHES AND NECTARINES

SERVING SIZE: 1 cup (145–175 grams)		CALORIES: 63–68
CARBS: 15–17 grams	PROTEIN: 2 grams	FAT: 0 grams

Why did we lump peaches and nectarines together? Well, despite being marketed as completely different fruits, peaches and nectarines actually belong to the same species. There are, of course, subtle differences: Peaches are sweeter, have a velvety skin and are not quite as nutritious as nectarines, which provide a bit more vitamin C, nearly double the vitamin A and more potassium (though both are solid sources of all three). In addition, both fruits provide some carbs, dietary fiber, vitamin E, niacin and vitamin K, which aids in strengthening your bones. Like most stone fruits, peaches and nectarines are high in sugars, and a few people may find the skins to cause allergic reactions.

PLUMS

SERVING SIZE: 1 cup (165 grams)		CALORIES: 76
CARBS: 19 grams	PROTEIN: 1 gram	FAT: 0 grams

Plums, whether in their raw or dried form, are excellent digestive aids and are even powerful laxatives. Their digestive properties come from dietary fibers and compounds such as sorbitol and isatin. Plums also contain vitamins A, C and K, making them good for overall health. One of the best things about plums is that they come in a variety of flavors and colors, ensuring that every plum-infused smoothie is a one-of-a-kind treat.

MELONS

You may not know it, but melons, like cantaloupe, watermelon and honeydew, are directly related to gourds like pumpkin, squash and zucchini, all of which are fruits of the Cucurbitales family despite often being treated as vegetables for culinary purposes. Melons don't tend to pack the same nutrient-rich punch as fruits like berries. They are, however, a wonderful way to add richly flavored liquid to otherwise dense smoothies.

CANTALOUPE

SERVING SIZE: 1 cup (177 grams)		CALORIES: 60
CARBS: 16 grams	PROTEIN: 1 gram	FAT: 0 grams

The delicate flesh and mild, sweet flavor of cantaloupe makes this melon a fantastic addition to any smoothie. Unlike other *super* fruits, cantaloupe doesn't have a significant broad range of nutrients; instead, it packs a punch of just a few. Surprisingly, a single serving of cantaloupe delivers 120 percent of your daily value of vitamin A and 108 percent of your daily value of vitamin C. It also can deliver as much as 14 percent of your daily potassium needs, as well as a gram of protein. Cantaloupe also has anti-inflammatory properties, which makes it a strong anti-cancer fruit, as well as a great addition to post-workout drinks.

HONEYDEW

SERVING SIZE: 1 cup (177 grams)		CALORIES: 60
CARBS: 16 grams	PROTEIN: 1 gram	FAT: 0 grams

Enjoy honeydew for its sweet, subtle flavor. The fact is, unlike other melons, honeydew is not a nutritional powerhouse. While it delivers about 50 percent of your daily vitamin C needs and 12 percent of your potassium, that's about all it has to offer. The carbohydrate balance isn't ideal either: The 16 grams of carbs in each serving are made up of just 2 grams are dietary fiber, and the other 14 grams are simple sugars. When it comes down to it, honeydew may be delicious, but there are other, healthier options.

WATERMELON

SERVING SIZE: 1 cup (154 grams)		CALORIES: 46
CARBS: 12 grams	PROTEIN: 1 gram	FAT: 0 grams

Watermelon is nature's (actually healthy) "vitamin water"! Containing an astounding 140 grams of water per serving, watermelon is the perfect thirst-quenching base for just about any summer smoothie. In addition to the delicately flavored water, watermelon is a great source of vitamin A (18 percent of daily value), vitamin C (21 percent of daily value), potassium (5 percent) and a gram of protein. Remember, while freezing watermelon can turn the flesh a bit mealy, the texture won't matter in a smoothie, so freezing cubes of watermelon is an excellent way to save a bit of summer for later in the year.

TROPICAL AND EXOTIC FRUITS

While many tropical and exotic fruits now grow in parts of the United States, most of these fruits have their genetic roots outside North America. And many of these fruits, such as the mango or papaya, grow best in the narrow geographical band between the Tropic of Cancer and the Tropic of Capricorn, where the equatorial sun allows for abundant growth. Some tropical and exotic fruits are revered as some of the best superfoods on the planet, while others are popular purely for their marvelous flavors. But regardless of their appeal, tropical and exotic fruits are a great way to give an otherwise normal smoothie a clever, colorful, nutritious and imported twist.

AÇAÍ

SERVING SIZE: 1 ounce (28 grams)		CALORIES: 20
CARBS: 1 gram	PROTEIN: 0 grams	FAT: 1 gram

This reddish, purple fruit found in the Amazon basin and throughout other rainforests of South and Central America, has become a superfood superstar, and for good reason: Açaí boasts more anthocyanins—powerful antioxidants that may help alleviate neurodegeneration, inflammation and pain— than any other known fruit. In addition to its high anthocyanin content, açaí is a good source of dietary fiber and the healthy fats, omega-3 fatty acids and omega-6 fatty acids. While açaí is undoubtedly healthy, some nutritionists caution that this fruit is no greater a superfood than your average high-antioxidant fruit, so paying exorbinant prices for the fruit may not be worth the cost. Even if açaí doesn't contain some secret super ingredient, it is still a healthy, delicious choice. Keep in mind that you are not likely to find fresh açaí, so look for freeze-dried fruit powder or packets of frozen açaí pulp to add to your smoothies.

COCONUT

COCONUT MEAT

SERVING SIZE: 1 cup (80 grams)		CALORIES: 283
CARBS: 12 grams	PROTEIN: 3 grams	FAT: 27 grams

COCONUT MILK

SERVING SIZE: 1 ounce (28 grams)		CALORIES: 64
CARBS: 2 grams	PROTEIN: 1 gram	FAT: 7 grams

COCONUT WATER

SERVING SIZE: 1 cup (237 grams)		CALORIES: 46
CARBS: 9 grams	PROTEIN: 2 grams	FAT: 0 grams

Because of their mineral-rich, ultra-replenishing "water," coconuts are a unique fruit; no other fruit contains a pure liquid portion (for more information on their hydrating and electrolyte benefits, see page 61). Coconuts are a wonderfully diverse equatorial fruit; in addition to the water, which is harvested from immature coconuts, coconuts are also cultivated for their "meat," the fleshy white part surrounding the water. Additionally, various parts of coconuts can be used to make coconut milk, coconut butter, coconut sugar and even coconut flour, a gluten-free flour alternative.

The coconut's various parts have different nutritional content. Coconut "meat," which is also pressed to produce coconut "milk," is very high in saturated fats and contains a lot of calories, but, while saturated fats can have negative effect on heart health, in moderate amounts it can be extremely beneficial to liver function, immunity and hormone production. In addition, this fatty meat is a good source of minerals, especially manganese, and to a lesser extent copper, selenium, iron, phosphorous and potassium. Coconut "water," the liquid at the center of the coconut, contains much less fat than the "meat" and has a higher concentration of vitamins, such as vitamin C and riboflavin. Like the meat, coconut water contains a plethora of minerals, including manganese, potassium, magnesium, calcium, iron and phosphorous.

WHO NEEDS GATORADE WHEN WE HAVE COCONUTS?

The advertising on all those little cartons of coconut water is no lie—these fruits are filled with electrolytes. But the benefits don't stop there: The chemical and mineral composition of coconuts are actually so close to that of human blood that they can theoretically serve as blood plasma replacements.

When added to a smoothie, in the forms of coconut water, milk, flesh or even oil, coconuts have a remarkably thirst-quenching and energizing effect. They also lend smoothies a taste of the tropics. They make the perfect addition to both before-, during- and after-workout smoothies.

KIWI

SERVING SIZE: 1 cup (175 grams)		CALORIES: 108
CARBS: 26 grams	PROTEIN: 2 grams	FAT: 1 gram

Originally known as "Chinese gooseberries," these delicious green fruits were renamed kiwis (or kiwifruit) after kiwis, the New Zealand national bird, because both are fury, small and brown. One hundred grams of kiwifruit contains a mind-boggling 155 percent daily value of vitamin C and 50 percent daily value of vitamin K. They are also a good source of vitamin E, vitamin B6, folate, calcium, magnesium, phosphorous, copper, manganese and 10 percent daily value of potassium. Surprisingly, two small kiwis contain more potassium then an entire banana.

MANGO

SERVING SIZE: 1 cup (165 grams)		CALORIES: 108
CARBS: 28 grams	PROTEIN: 1 gram	FAT: 0 grams

The mango is one of the most popular exotic fruits for a reason. Known in some parts of the world as "the king of fruits," the mango has properties that can help improve vision and help prevent cancer. Low in calories and high in nutrients, 100 grams of mango contains about a quarter your daily value of vitamin A in the form of beta-carotene, making it an ideal smoothie addition if you're looking to sharpen your eyesight. Mangoes also contain nearly half your daily value of vitamin C, and they contain unique antioxidants such as quercetin, isoquercitrin, astragalin, fisetin, gallic acid and methyl gallat—giving mangoes their immune system–boosting and cancer-preventing qualities. The only cautions you need to take with mangoes are with the high sugar content and allergens in the skin of the fruit that can give you a rash, something to look out for during peeling and prep, particularly if you are susceptible to poison oak or ivy infections.

PAPAYA

SERVING SIZE: 1 cup (140 grams)		CALORIES: 55
CARBS: 14 grams	PROTEIN: 1 gram	FAT: 0 grams

Papayas seem to have a polarizing flavor profile; some people hate them, while others think there's no tastier fruit. Whichever camp you fall into, know that the papaya is one of the healthiest fruits on earth, with high levels of antioxidants such as provitamin A caretonoids and phytochemicals. A hundred grams—less than a single small papaya—contains over 100 percent of your daily value of vitamin C and about 22 percent of your daily value of vitamin A, and is an excellent source of papain, a powerful digestive aid. Papayas are also a good source of dietary fiber, folate, potassium, vitamin K and vitamin E, and play an integral role in traditional medicine, with uses ranging from treatment of cuts, burns and rashes (when used as an ointment) to prevention and treatment of fungal infections. It's important to point out that about 80 percent of Hawaiian papayas are considered GMOs—they've been genetically modified to resist papaya ringspot virus, which in the 1980s and 1990s threatened to eliminate the entire Hawaiian crop.

PINEAPPLE

SERVING SIZE: 1 cup (165 grams)		CALORIES: 82
CARBS: 22 grams	PROTEIN: 1 gram	FAT: 0 grams

This delicious and popular tropical fruit, which is notable for its subtle sweet and tart balance, is a colorful and nutritious addition to most smoothies. The pineapple is an excellent source of vitamin C and a superior source of manganese. It also contains vitamin B6, copper, potassium, magnesium, folate and thiamin. Pineapples are also the world's only source of bromelain, an anti-inflammatory that's been used to help treat arthritis. However, bromelain may not be present in useful doses in the fruit, but the extract is widely available.

STAR FRUIT

SERVING SIZE: 1 cup (132 grams)		CALORIES: 41
CARBS: 9 grams	PROTEIN: 1 gram	FAT: 0 grams

The carambola, colloquially known as the star fruit because of its unique shape, is a popular fruit throughout Southeast Asia, East Asia and the Pacific Islands. A hundred grams of the star-shaped fruit contains nearly 60 percent of your daily value of vitamin C and is also a solid source of dietary fibers, potassium, copper and folate. It is rich in polyphenolic antioxidants, which may help in preventing heart disease and lowering bad cholesterol. The star fruit comes in two varieties: Smaller ones are sour and tangy, while the larger carambolas are richer and sweeter. The edible skin is crunchy, while the fleshy interior is juicy and soft, like a grape. Taste-wise, star fruits range from "crisp green apple" to "sweet citrus." Star fruits, especially the sour varietals, contain oxalic acid, which can be dangerous for those with kidney problems. Star fruit also contains compounds that can interact dangerously with certain medications such as statins and benzodiazapines.

SAVORY FRUITS

Did you know that the tomato is the state vegetable of New Jersey? It's also the state fruit of Ohio...and both the state fruit *and* the state vegetable of Arkansas. But while the tomato, cucumber and avocado are often misidentified as vegetables, their nutritional content and natural classification is all fruit. But whatever you call them, thanks to lower sugar levels and excellent nutritional make up, these so-called savory fruits make for excellent additions to any fruit or green smoothie.

AVOCADO

SERVING SIZE: 1 cup (150 grams)		CALORIES: 240
CARBS: 13 grams	PROTEIN: 3 grams	FAT: 22 grams

It can take a leap of faith, but avocados are actually a wonderful smoothie ingredient, especially if you're looking for something that's at once filling, delicious and very healthy. Loaded with 4 grams of protein and even some essential omega fats, avocados are one of the most substantial of all fruits and vegetables. But they're also filled with vitamins and minerals. One hundred grams of avocado supplies 17 percent of your daily value of vitamin C, 26 percent of your vitamin K, 13 percent of your vitamin B6, 20 percent of your folate and 27 percent of your daily dietary fiber. The benefits don't stop there: Avocados are also good sources of potassium, manganese, magnesium, copper, zinc, phosphorus and iron—basically every vital mineral but calcium. Avocados can balance both savory and sweet dishes; in fact, avocado milkshakes sprinkled with chocolate syrup are a popular dessert throughout Southeast Asia—try some of our avocado dessert smoothies as a post-workout, pre-bedtime power boost.

CUCUMBER

SERVING SIZE: 1 cup (52 grams)		CALORIES: 8
CARBS: 2 grams	PROTEIN: 0 grams	FAT: 0 grams

When you think of a cold, crisp, cucumber, words like "refreshing" and "hydrating" probably come to mind. That's because cucumbers are about 95 percent water! They do contain some of those life-affirming vitamins and minerals; they're a good source of vitamin K, and provide moderate amounts of vitamin C, vitamin A, pantothenic acid, potassium, magnesium and manganese. Cucumbers are also one of the only sources of the aptly named cucurbitcins, unique phytonutrients that may have anti-cancer benefits. Because of their mild, refreshing flavor profile, cucumbers are a subtle, hydrating addition to any green smoothie, and work well when paired with substantial, creamy fruits like mango or papaya.

TOMATO

SERVING SIZE: 1 cup (149 grams)		CALORIES: 27
CARBS: 6 grams	PROTEIN: 1 gram	FAT: 0 grams

We're the first to admit that the words "tomato" and "smoothie" don't make the most natural-sounding pairing. But the fact is that a handful of juicy Red Cherry, Campari or Grape tomatoes can add a subtle, healthy twist to any number of green and fruit smoothies. Tomatoes have loads of vitamin C, vitamin A, vitamin K and potassium, and are decent sources of dietary fiber, vitamin E, niacin, vitamin B6, folate, copper and manganese. But their real secret lies in the antioxidant lycopene, which is found in all 6,500 tomato varieties and a handful of other red fruits and vegetables such as watermelon and pink grapefruit. Although inconclusive, research has shown that a diet rich in lycopene may be helpful in preventing prostate and other cancers. In smoothies, tomatoes should be used in moderation and should be combined with a sweet, flavorful fruit and a dominant liquid base.

NATURAL SWEETENERS

The sad fact is that there really is no such thing as a *healthy* natural sweetener. Whether you're a proponent of agave, honey, maple syrup or plain table sugar, you're always going to be consuming the same "bad" thing—simple, sweet carbohydrates—and not much else. That being said, a small dash of honey or agave in your healthy green smoothie can make all the difference taste-wise; and if the choice is between developing a healthy smoothie habit or saving those extra 64 calories, you should sweeten it up! Of course, if you can get away with it, we highly suggest substituting in fruits as your natural sweetener instead.

HONEY

SERVING SIZE: 1 tablespoon (21 grams)	CALORIES: 64	
CARBS: 17 grams	PROTEIN: 0 grams	FAT: 0 grams

Taste-wise, honey, naturally made by bees from the nectar of plants, is one of nature's most wonderful sweeteners. While honey has trace amounts of protein, nutrients and vitamins (like vitamin C and iron), it is not actually a significant source of anything but simple carbohydrates like glucose and fructose. It is, in other words, more or less empty calories. That being said, a tablespoon of honey will go a long way towards making your smoothie more enjoyable, without doing much damage. Compared to simple table sugar, honey offers a touch of nutrition and fewer carbs (17 grams in a tablespoon of honey compared to 24 grams in a tablespoon of sugar). Darker varieties like buckwheat have also been shown to harbor some antioxidants.

AGAVE SYRUP

SERVING SIZE: 1 tablespoon (20 grams)		CALORIES: 64
CARBS: 17 grams	PROTEIN: 0 grams	FAT: 0 grams

Over the last several years, agave has rocketed in popularity as a safe and natural alternative to sugar, stevia, artificial sweeteners and the like. Don't be fooled—there's nothing particularly incredible about agave in any form. Derived from the same monocot plant used to produce tequila (another not-so-healthy product) agave syrup or nectar is considered "better for you" than table sugar for one simple reason—it's actually sweeter than cane sugar. And that means that to get the same potency of sweetness, you end up using less agave syrup than you would table sugar. Agave is also very high in fructose, the same vilified simple sugar contained within high-fructose corn syrup. Consumed in high amounts in sweeteners (not whole fruit!), this sugar has been linked to weight gain.

FOUR

GREENS, HERBS, SPROUTS AND ALGAE

GREENS

Leafy green vegetables are popular. There's no doubt about that. These ultra-nutritious superfoods are popping up everywhere from restaurant menus and grocery stores to bottled juices and even protein bars. And the reputation they've built in the health community is well deserved—leafy greens truly are life-changing and life-saving foods. Devoid of fats but still packing complex carbohydrates and protein, these easy-to-blend veggies are nutrient powerhouses. Most of the greens on this list will deliver an entire day's worth of vitamin A (which improves skin health and can fight cancer), vitamin C (which promotes the immune system) and vitamin K (which can increase bone strength). In addition, growing straight from the mineral-rich earth, the greens will keep your body flush with calcium, copper, iron, phosphorus, potassium, magnesium, manganese and zinc, all of which help maintain a healthy, working body. Adding veggies to an already-delicious fruit smoothie may sound a little intimidating, but just remember—a little bit of green goes a long, long way.

BEET GREENS

SERVING SIZE: 1 cup (38 grams)		CALORIES: 8
CARBS: 2 grams	PROTEIN: 1 gram	FAT: 0 grams

Beet greens, the leafy above-ground counterpart to the more recognizable subterranean root vegetable, are a highly nutritious and fairly mild option for turning your fruit smoothie green. The greens are loaded with vitamins A and K and provide about a quarter of your daily value of vitamin C. They also provide a good source of calcium and potassium, and a small quantity of omega fats and complete protein. The one drawback to beet greens is their somewhat-high sodium content; a single serving has as much as 5 percent of your daily allotted sodium intake—although this can make them an ideal post-workout addition to a recovery smoothie to help replenish salt lost during exercise.

CHARD

SERVING SIZE: 1 cup (36 grams)		CALORIES: 7
CARBS: 1 gram	PROTEIN: 1 gram	FAT: 0 grams

Tough and hearty, raw Swiss chard is not the most intuitive addition to the smoothie mix, but it is a very healthy one. A single cup serving provides an astounding 375 percent of your daily vitamin K needs along with hefty doses of vitamins A, B6, C and E. On the mineral side, chard offers decent quantities of calcium, iron, magnesium, potassium, manganese and zinc. Chard's single gram of protein per serving has eight of the nine essential amino acids, making it a great addition to a post-workout smoothie.

DANDELION GREENS

SERVING SIZE: 1 cup (55 grams)		CALORIES: 25
CARBS: 5 grams	PROTEIN: 1 gram	FAT: 0 grams

Considered an invasive weed in most gardens, dandelion greens just so happen to be an incredibly nutritious, edible green. Their fairly smooth consistency when blended, coupled with a sharp tangy-bordering-on-spicy flavor, makes them a bold addition to any smoothie. Nutrient-wise, dandelion greens boast over 100 percent of your daily vitamin A needs and well over 500 percent of your vitamin K. The greens also offer good servings of vitamin C, B6 and E, as well as riboflavin and folate. Dandelion greens pack nearly 10 percent of your daily calcium and iron needs and have trace amounts of magnesium, potassium, manganese and zinc to go along with 1 gram of protein per one-cup serving.

KALE

SERVING SIZE: 1 cup (67 grams)		CALORIES: 33
CARBS: 7 grams	PROTEIN: 2 grams	FAT: 1 gram

Kale, the leafy green relative of broccoli, cabbage and brussels sprouts, is the very definition of superfood. A serving of raw, fresh kale impressively packs well over 100 percent of your daily value of vitamins A, C and K. The benefits don't stop there—these simple greens are also chock-full of calcium, iron, magnesium, potassium and dietary fiber, and even offer 2 grams of protein per serving. In addition kale is highly anti-inflammatory, which can help prevent or reduce post-workout muscle inflammation. While the leaves are rugged and may take a little longer to blend than average lettuces or spinach, the health benefits are worth the trouble.

SPINACH

SERVING SIZE: 1 cup (30 grams)		CALORIES: 7
CARBS: 1 gram	PROTEIN: 1 gram	FAT: 0 grams

Spinach, like so many of the other leafy greens, is an incredible nutritional powerhouse. In addition to a full gram of complete protein, a cup of spinach provides big doses of all your fat-soluble vitamins necessary for bone strength, skin health and vision, including 180 percent of your daily recommended vitamin K, 35 percent of your vitamin E and 56 percent of your vitamin A. In addition, a handful of spinach in your smoothie will give it an infusion of iron, folate and vitamin C. Possibly most important, however, is the superior taste and texture that spinach can give any smoothie. Spinach has a delicate flavor and blends superbly, giving smoothies a creamy green texture without really affecting the taste. So, if you're having trouble getting used to throwing kale or collards into your favorite fruit smoothie, we suggest mixing your greens with 50 percent spinach.

HERBS, SPROUTS AND...ALGAE?

Select herbs, sprouts and algae also make nutritious additions to your green smoothies, especially if you're looking to add protein, increase your smoothie's cleansing effects or just want to spice things up a bit. Herbs such as basil, cilantro, mint and parsley have powerful detoxifying properties that help your body wash out the bad and replace it with the good. Sprouts such as alfalfa are packed with nutrients, have a subtle, fun flavor and are relatively inexpensive. Algae, specifically the wonder food spirulina, is a modern smoothie staple thanks to its animal-free protein, naturally occurring phytonutrients and rich chlorophyll.

ALFALFA SPROUTS

SERVING SIZE: 1 cup (33 grams)		CALORIES: 8
CARBS: 1 gram	PROTEIN: 1 gram	FAT: 0 grams

Alfalfa sprouts make a powerful, high-protein, low-calorie addition to an assortment of smoothies. One hundred grams of sprouts (which, should be noted, is almost three cups) contain only 23 calories yet provides nearly 10 percent of your daily protein needs. Alfalfa sprouts are also a very good source of vitamins A, C and K. Additionally, they contain moderate amounts of thiamin, riboflavin, folate, pantothenic acid, calcium, iron, magnesium, phosphorus, zinc, copper and manganese. Alfalfa sprouts have been used in traditional Chinese medicine for millennia to alleviate kidney and digestive problems, however, note that the seeds of the sprout contain an amino acid known as canavanine, which in high doses can lead to lupus or arthritis-like symptoms.

BASIL

SERVING SIZE: 5 leaves (about ⅛ cup or 2 grams)		CALORIES: 1
CARBS: 0 grams	PROTEIN: 0 grams	FAT: 0 grams

Commonly used as an herb to enhance the flavor of many savory dishes, basil comes in many different varieties, all of them flavorful. In normal doses, basil is a good source of vitamins K and A, and in large doses it also provides a decent source of manganese, copper, magnesium, iron, calcium, vitamin B6, vitamin C and protein. But it's basil's essential oils—what gives it its unique aroma—that provide the real health benefits as a powerful anti-bacterial and anti-microbal food source. In your smoothies, it's best to use fresh basil (although frozen and dried can both be used).

MINT

SERVING SIZE: 20 leaves (1 gram)		CALORIES: 2
CARBS: 1 gram	PROTEIN: 0 gram	FAT: 0 grams

Mint makes a fantastic, mild-to-flavorful addition to smoothies. Mint comes in a wide variety of species, most commonly spearmint and peppermint, and each species has its own unique taste. In general, mints are good sources of vitamin A, vitamin C, riboflavin, folate, iron, magnesium, potassium, calcium and manganese, and, like most herbs, have essential oils that provide substantial health benefits. For example, the menthol in peppermint (and to a lesser extent the carvone in spearmint) provides a natural remedy for stomach problems such as indigestion, irritable bowel syndrome and gas.

PARSLEY

SERVING SIZE: 1 cup chopped sprigs (60 grams)		CALORIES: 22
CARBS: 4 grams	PROTEIN: 2 grams	FAT: 0 grams

Parsley is a super-healthy herb that aids in digestion and can add a unique twist to a variety of savory smoothie blends. It's rich in flavonoids and antioxidants, including lutein and zeaxanthin, which can aid in vision. Parsley is also a good source of folate, vitamin K, vitamin C and vitamin A.

SPIRULINA

SERVING SIZE: 1 ounce (28 grams)		CALORIES: 7
CARBS: 1 gram	PROTEIN: 2 grams	FAT: 0 grams

The superfood sprirulina, composed of two types of tropical/ subtropical freshwater cyanobacteria, is an incredibly nutritious, protein-heavy "blue-green algae" that can be bought in pill or powder form. Taken alone, spirulina can have an overpowering seaweed flavor, making smoothies a great way to get the health benefits while masking the potent taste. But if you can get used to it, spirulina makes for a great exercise booster as it is one of the only plant-derived foods that provides every essential amino acid, making it a complete protein (though expensive and in fairly low quantity compared to other protein sources). It's also an excellent source of thiamine, riboflavin, iron, manganese and magnesium, and is a very good source of niacin, pantothenic acid, vitamin B6, vitamin E, vitamin K, calcium and phosphorus.

FIVE

STARCHES, GRAINS, SEEDS AND NUTS

In addition to being superfoods on their own (like quinoa and sweet potatoes), starches, grains, seeds and nuts can add a whole other level to your smoothies—thickening their consistency, providing additional complex carbohydrates for energy and even boosting the protein content through all-natural, healthy plant proteins. Keep in mind that using starches, grains and seeds often comes with preparation time—you may need to boil, cook or soak these ingredients to make them work in your smoothies.

STARCHES

PLANTAINS

SERVING SIZE: 1 cup (200 grams)		CALORIES: 232
CARBS: 62 grams	PROTEIN: 2 grams	FAT: 0 grams

Unlike bananas cooked in desserts, cooked plantains are an excellent source of complex carbohydrates (62 grams per serving), making them ideal for carb-loading smoothies. While plantains offer a good source of vitamin A (36 percent) and vitamin C (36 percent), most of the water-soluble vitamins will be degraded when the plantain is cooked—which you may want to do before consuming, depending on the ripeness. Therefore, it's best to use plantains primarily as a rich source of complex carbs (and complete protein) in addition to nutrient-rich fruits and vegetables. As far as smoothies go, you should boil plantains that still have a yellow skin before adding them to your smoothies; while the process eliminates much of the flavor, the dense flesh of the plantains will add a wonderful, filling thickness to any smoothie. Plantains with a significant amount of black on their skin can be used raw in smoothies, much like regular bananas.

SWEET POTATOES

SERVING SIZE: 1 cup (200 grams)		CALORIES: 180
CARBS: 41 grams	PROTEIN: 4 grams	FAT: 0 grams

It may sound a bit counterintuitive to add sweet potato to your smoothies, but be assured it can make an excellent base for thick, filling smoothies. Long heralded as one of the world's top superfoods, sweet potatoes offer a myriad of health benefits. Number one is beta-carotene (which gives them their rich orange flesh), sweet potatoes offer over 700 percent of your daily value of vitamin A in every serving. In addition, they are an excellent source of vitamin C (65 percent), vitamin B6 (29 percent), magnesium (14 percent), potassium (27 percent), copper (16 percent) and manganese (50 percent). In addition to the high nutrient content, sweet potatoes are superb carb-loading ingredients—in a single serving, they offer nearly 7 grams of dietary fiber and 14 grams of complex carbohydrates (in addition to healthy omega-6 fats and 4 grams of protein!). The best way to use sweet potatoes in your smoothie making is to bake a sweet potato raw, in its own skin, the night before making your smoothie. Refrigerate the baked sweet potato overnight and then use the cool, cooked flesh for days afterward.

GRAINS

OATS

SERVING SIZE: 3 tablespoons to ¼ cup (28 grams)	CALORIES: 109	
CARBS: 19 grams	PROTEIN: 5 grams	FAT: 2 grams

Any breakfast cereal that's a favorite of the Scottish Highlanders has got to have some serious health benefits. Turns out, rolled oats earn that reputation. Packed with complex carbohydrates, oatmeal is the ultimate athlete's grain, allowing the body to balance its blood-glucose levels and encouraging a slow, steady digestive process. In addition, oats are chock-full of B1 and B2 vitamins, giving you an extra boost of energy along with a boost of good carbs.

The easiest way to add them to your smoothies is to cook the oats hot and then let them cool to around room temperature. In the smoothie, they'll add a nutty taste and thicken the consistency. Drink an oat smoothie and you'll feel like you're having a whole meal.

SEEDS

QUINOA

SERVING SIZE: 3 tablespoons to ¼ cup (28 grams)		**CALORIES:** 103
CARBS: 18 grams	**PROTEIN:** 4 grams	**FAT:** 2 grams

Quinoa, a staple "grain" of South America, is one of the world's best sources of plant-based protein as it is actually a seed. A single one-cup serving of uncooked quinoa delivers 24 grams of complete protein. Of course, you won't want to put a full cup of quinoa in *any* smoothie. Still, an ounce of uncooked quinoa will thicken up any watery smoothie and infuse it with 4 grams of complete protein along with plenty of iron, magnesium, folate and manganese.

CHIA SEEDS

SERVING SIZE: 3 tablespoons to ¼ cup (28 grams)		**CALORIES:** 137
CARBS: 12 grams	**PROTEIN:** 4 grams	**FAT:** 9 grams

Chia seeds, the miracle food of the Aztecs, are rapidly rising in popularity. The seeds offer an excellent nutritional balance in 140 calories per serving, including 9 grams of healthy fats, 4 grams of complete protein, 18 percent of your daily calcium intake needs and 10 grams of dietary fiber. Unlike common grains like wheat, chia seeds are also anti-inflammatory, which makes them a perfect carb source for daily smoothies. Chia seeds can be soaked before adding them to your smoothie (they'll blend smoothly) or added them whole, raw and dried for added texture. Either way, the seeds will add a very palatable thickness to any smoothie that's a little runny.

FLAXSEEDS

SERVING SIZE: 3 tablespoons to ¼ cup (28 grams)		CALORIES: 150
CARBS: 8 grams	PROTEIN: 5 grams	FAT: 12 grams

Although flax has only recently risen to prominence in the health world, its wondrous properties have been known for thousands of years. Flax, also known by artists as linseed, is a flowering annual plant that has been cultivated since man first settled in the Fertile Crescent perhaps 10,000 years ago. Both the plant and the seeds are excellent sources of fiber. In addition, the seeds offer a superb source of plant-derived omega-3 fatty acids and lignans, antioxidants that may protect the body from developing certain types of cancers. In addition to having a perfect complete protein profile (and offering 5 grams of protein per 1 ounce serving), an ounce of flaxseed has 31 percent of your daily value of thiamin, 9 percent of your daily iron requirement, 27 percent of your daily value of magnesium and 17 percent of your copper. Flaxseed is also a strong anti-inflammatory ingredient, perfect for a post-workout smoothie blend.

HEMP SEEDS

SERVING SIZE: 3 tablespoons to ¼ cup (28 grams)	CALORIES: 170
CARBS: 3 grams	PROTEIN: 10 grams	FAT: 13 grams

Though often associated with its psychoactive cousin, marijuana, hemp has no drug-like effects and the seeds of the plant are extremely nutritious, widely available and will offer your smoothies a pleasing, mild, nutty flavor. Hemp seeds are an excellent source of protein with about 10 grams (containing all nine essential amino acids) in a single ounce, about three tablespoons' worth. Hemp seeds are solid sources of fiber and vitamin E, and offer healthy doses of both omega-3 and omega-6 fatty acids. Furthermore, most people find hemp easy to digest. Unlike supplements like whey and casein, most people will not experience bloating when using ground hemp seed as a protein booster in smoothies.

NUTS

There's a reason nuts are a huge portion of almost every trail mix: Nuts are packed with protein and essential fats, so they tend to be the perfect snack if you are prepping—or in the middle of—an arduous workout. If the words "essential" and "fats" strike you as an oxymoron, rest assured that the fats contained in nuts tend to be the ones that humans need to survive, such as omega-3 fatty acids, omega-6 fatty acids and unsaturated fats such as monounsaturated fats, which help prevent heart disease by lowering cholesterol levels. In fact, some studies show that a diet rich in nuts can actually help you lose weight!

In addition, most nuts have antioxidant levels rivaling those of fruits and are also an excellent source of dietary fiber. If you are the type who enjoys a snack in between meals, switching from unhealthy processed snack foods to nutrient-dense nuts has been scientifically proven capable of adding years onto your life span. Consumed in moderation, nuts can take your smoothie to the next level: Their protein and fat contents provide you with longer-lasting energy, and they can give any smoothie a subtle, nutty flavor spin. If you don't have a top-dollar blender, try softening your nuts by soaking them in water for about 8 hours before blending (be sure to discard the soak water).

ALMONDS

SERVING SIZE: 3 tablespoons to ¼ cup (28 grams)		CALORIES: 167
CARBS: 5 grams	PROTEIN: 6 grams	FAT: 15 grams

Almonds are an excellent choice if you're trying to maintain your weight: Despite being high in fats, studies show that almonds, when paired with a low-calorie diet, can help you lose weight and keep it off. A single serving of almonds contains about a third of your daily values of manganese and vitamin E, a powerful antioxidant. Almonds are also a good source of protein, dietary fibers, riboflavin, magnesium, phosphorus and copper, while providing trace levels of zinc, potassium, iron, calcium, niacin, folate and thiamin. Finally, almonds contain significant amounts of phytosterols, steroid compounds found in plants that can help lower your cholesterol. Almonds are one of the known food allergens, so be wary when making almond-flavored smoothies for your friends and acquaintances.

PEANUTS

SERVING SIZE: 3 tablespoons to ¼ cup (28 grams)		CALORIES: 149
CARBS: 5 grams	PROTEIN: 7 grams	FAT: 14 grams

So, they're not really nuts (peanuts, like beans, are legumes) but peanuts are a veritable cornucopia of protein, dietary fibers, good fats, antioxidants, vitamins and minerals, making them an excellent energy-boosting pre- or post-workout snack. Specifically, peanuts are a good source of vitamin E, thiamin, niacin, folate, magnesium, phosphorus, copper, as well as 27 percent your daily value of manganese. In addition, peanuts have trace amounts of vitamin B6, riboflavin, calcium, selenium, iron and zinc. Peanuts also contain resveratrol, which is a chemical compound that may reduce your risk for cancer and heart disease.

As much as 2 percent of the population may be allergic to peanuts, and some reactions include anaphylactic shock, which can lead to death. In fact, some people have such powerful allergies that peanuts and peanut butter have been banned in many schools and were even considered being removed from airlines! Another potential pitfall of peanuts is that they are absolutely loaded with calories (159 per ounce), so eat them in moderation.

WALNUTS

SERVING SIZE: 3 tablespoons to ¼ cup (28 grams)	CALORIES: 183	
CARBS: 4 grams	PROTEIN: 4 grams	FAT: 18 grams

Walnuts are an impressive nut, packing more antioxidants and more omega-3 fatty acids, a powerful anti-inflammatory, than any other nut. Walnuts are an ideal ingredient for those suffering from joint or back pain who don't want to miss a workout. Walnuts also contain about half your daily value of manganese and 22 percent of your daily value of copper. Walnuts also contain thiamin, vitamin B6, folate, phosphorus, zinc, potassium, iron, calcium, selenium, pantothenic acid, dietary fiber and magnesium, which helps in energy production and muscle function. Because walnuts, like most nuts, are high in fats (albeit good fats!), you should enjoy them in moderation, about an ounce or two daily.

CASHEWS

SERVING SIZE: 3 tablespoons to ¼ cup (28 grams)	CALORIES: 161	
CARBS: 9 grams	PROTEIN: 4 grams	FAT: 13 grams

Cashews are a great nut-lover's choice for those of us watching our weight, as they contain a little less fat than your average nut while still being loaded with tons of protein and antioxidants. Cashews are also bursting with crucial minerals such as iron and zinc, the latter of which is vital for normal cell function and can even maintain proper smell and taste functioning (so you can keep enjoying your cashew smoothies!). Cashews also contain solid amounts of vitamin K, thiamin, niacin, vitamin

B6, folate pantothenic acid, dietary fiber, carbohydrates, magnesium, phosphorus, potassium, copper, manganese and selenium. Cashews do, however, contain oxalates, which can be dangerous for those with unmedicated kidney or gallbladder problems.

SIX

PROTEIN AND OTHER SMOOTHIE SUPPLEMENTS

What is protein and why is it so important? Proteins are combinations of amino acids, organic compounds based around the primary bond of amine and carboxylic acid. Plants and animals use these strings of amino acids, in the form of proteins, to build cells, enzymes, tissue and muscle. Proteins are thus the very building blocks of material life.

Most plants and animals can synthesize many of the amino acids they need on their own, without consuming any outside sources. Humans, on the other hand, need a bit of help from their diet to synthesize all 22 necessary amino acids in order to keep the body growing and developing throughout the human lifetime. These "missing" amino acids are commonly referred to as the "nine essential amino acids" and include histidine, isoleucine, leucine, lysine, methionine, phenylalanine, threonine, tryptophan and valine. Feeding your body these necessary amino acids is really what nutrition is all about. While many foods have some of the essential amino acids, there are several "complete protein" sources—one-stop sources for all of them. For smoothie-making purposes, these include milk, soy, eggs, hemp seeds, chia seeds, quinoa and spirulina. Of course, not every complete protein is created equal, and some pack more protein punch than others.

The average person requires between 45 and 55 grams of protein each day to help repair the everyday wear and tear on the body. But athletes, who do significantly more daily strain to muscles and tissues, should be consuming an average of 70–80 grams of protein. Athletes and bodybuilders looking to dramatically increase muscle mass can up their daily protein intake to 100–110 grams.

Below is a table and outline of different protein sources. Note that macronutrient content may vary from brand to brand. The figures here are provided as best estimates based on official government information.

DAIRY AND POWDER PROTEIN SOURCES AT A GLANCE*

PROTEIN SOURCE	SERVING	CALORIES	CARBS	PROTEINS	FATS
Whole-Fat Greek Yogurt	1 cup	175	7	15	11
Low-Fat Cottage Cheese	1 cup	144	6	24	2
Egg White Powder Supplement	1 scoop	105	1	23	0
Whey Supplement	1 scoop	120	3	24	1
Casein Supplement	1 scoop	120	3	24	1
Soy Supplement	1 scoop	95	2	23	1
Mixed-Plant Supplement (Vega One)	1 scoop	140	12	15	3
Mixed-Plant Supplement (Vega Sport)	1 scoop	127	4.5	25	2
Rice Protein Supplement	1 scoop	60	2	12	0
Whole-Fat Dairy Milk	1 cup	146	13	8	8

* Macronutrient counts may vary depending on your preferred brand or type (i.e., low-fat, fortified, etc.)

DAIRY-BASED PROTEIN SOURCES

GREEK YOGURT (WHOLE FAT)

SERVING SIZE: 1 cup (200 grams)		CALORIES: 130
CARBS: 5 grams	PROTEIN: 11 grams	FAT: 8 grams

Whether you're looking to pack on some muscle or lose weight, Greek yogurt is a delicious, creamy way of achieving your goals as well as thickening your favorite smoothies. The recent Greek yogurt revolution is happening for a reason—compared to regular, old-fashioned yogurt, Greek yogurt is the healthier, leaner choice. Its secret is in the production: Greek yogurt, also known as strained yogurt, is made by filtering regular yogurt through meshed material like muslin cloth. This straining process rids the yogurt of lactose and much of the liquid whey, leaving a casein-protein-rich yogurt with less sugar, sodium and simple carbs. With a yogurt creamier, twice as high in protein and half as high in sugar, you have an ideal additive to any smoothie for bodybuilders and weight watchers alike. As far as the nitty-gritty numbers go, a typical 5.3-ounce (150 gram) serving of plain Greek yogurt contains between 80 and 130 calories and provides up to 20 grams of protein (compared to 9 grams of protein in regular yogurts). Greek yogurt also contains probiotics, beneficial bacteria that may have wide-ranging health benefits such as improved digestion, improved immune functioning, lowered cholesterol and reduced inflammation. It should be noted that Greek yogurt contains less lactose than regular yogurt, but is far from lactose-free. And Greek yogurt isn't perfect; it's lower in calcium than traditional yogurts; and full-fat versions can have a significant amount of saturated fat.

We highly suggest adding plain Greek yogurt to your smoothies as opposed to flavored options. Plain yogurt is generally the healthiest, offering you maximum protein without the sugar overload of flavored yogurts.

COTTAGE CHEESE (LOW-FAT)

SERVING SIZE: ½ cup (100 grams)		CALORIES: 72
CARBS: 3 grams	PROTEIN: 12 grams	FAT: 1 gram

Like Greek yogurt, cottage cheese is a beloved food for people looking to both lose weight and build muscle. One hundred grams of low-fat cottage cheese contains about 12 grams of protein (25 percent your daily value), while only containing about 90 calories (4 percent of your daily value). In particular, cottage cheese is an excellent natural source of casein protein, which bodybuilders and endurance athletes love because it provides the body with slower-digesting protein for more prolonged muscle growth. Cottage cheese is also a good source of calcium, phosphorous and vitamin A, but is also very high in sodium. Some people find the texture of cottage cheese alone to be unappealing. Even if you're in that camp, we suggest you give cottage cheese a try in a smoothie—blended, cottage cheese can give your smoothies a texture similar to a milkshake!

EGG WHITES

SERVING SIZE: ½ cup (120 grams)		CALORIES: 59
CARBS: 1 gram	PROTEIN: 13 grams	FAT: 0 grams

Surrounding the calorie-rich yellow yolk of an egg is one of nature's richest sources of protein. Egg whites are low-fat, low-cholesterol and best of all low cost compared to other protein options. In nature, the gelatinous white of a developing egg is designed to be the food source for the growing embryo. The egg white from one large egg contains about 3.6 grams of protein (7 percent of your recommended daily intake), and contains potassium and selenium, which aids in thyroid and immune function. Egg whites are easy to separate from the yolks: Simply crack the shell over a bowl, and then pass the yolk back and forth between the two shell halves, letting the egg whites cascade downward into a bowl below. If that sounds like too much work and you can afford to spend a little extra, you can always buy pre-separated egg whites by the carton or jar. They are pasteurized, meaning you can safely add them straight from the carton into the blender.

DAIRY-BASED PROTEIN SUPPLEMENTS

WHEY PROTEIN SUPPLEMENT

SERVING SIZE: 1 scoop (28–34 grams)		CALORIES: 120
CARBS: 3 grams	PROTEIN: 24 grams	FAT: 1 gram

Whey is no novel, synthetic invention of the fitness industry—it's actually the byproduct of cheese making. One of milk's two primary proteins, whey is a highly efficient (it contains every amino acid required for muscle repair and production), easily digestible (there's virtually no lactose) and healthy protein option for those athletes looking to rapidly gain muscle. In addition to its strength-building properties, whey can also help you lose weight and prevent diseases like osteoporosis, heart disease and asthma.

When choosing a whey supplement, be sure to check the WPC (whey protein concentrate) level. Supplements can range from high-fat, low-protein (30 percent) combinations to near pure (90 percent) protein formulas like whey protein isolates.

Be aware that whey does come with some potential side effects. Because it's a milk-based product, whey can cause cramping and upset stomach in some people.

CASEIN PROTEIN SUPPLEMENT

SERVING SIZE: 1 scoop (28–34 grams)		CALORIES: 120
CARBS: 3 grams	PROTEIN: 24 grams	FAT: 1 gram

Drink a glass of milk or a serving of yogurt and the main protein you're consuming is casein. This superb protein makes up 75–85 percent of the protein content of milk and provides you with an extremely efficient source of slow-digesting protein composed of a complex structure of amino acids and unique peptides (short-chain amino acids). What makes casein a particularly interesting and effective protein source is that it is water-insoluble. In its natural state, casein actually remains suspended within the surrounding milk, incapable of mixing with the liquid. And as a supplement, consuming casein powder will cause it to form a small, gelatinous clump in your stomach, which allows your digestive system to synthesize it over the course of a number of hours. This natural time-releasing quality makes it the perfect addition to a midday smoothie or nighttime blend, feeding your body ample protein between meals. Because casein protein is water-insoluble, keep in mind that you should consume it in moderation since your body is not efficient at flushing out any excess protein. If you are consuming the recommended doses, you should not have any problems.

EGG PROTEIN SUPPLEMENT

SERVING SIZE: 1 scoop (28–34 grams)		**CALORIES:** 130
CARBS: 5 grams	**PROTEIN:** 24 grams	**FAT:** 1 gram

Egg protein, either made from the nutrient-rich whites of eggs or the whole egg itself, is a good supplement option for any athlete trying to maximize muscle growth without consuming products made from cow milk. The supplements on the market are generally low-fat, low-cholesterol and offer a complete source of all nine essential amino acids in a standard concentration of 25 grams of protein per serving. Unlike casein or whey supplements, egg protein supplements don't carry the same milk-related allergens and are generally a bit easier for the body to digest. Of course, egg whites come with their own potential allergy problems, so consult your doctor if you have any concerns prior to trying a new supplement.

PLANT-BASED SUPPLEMENTS

More and more athletes are gravitating toward using plant protein supplements over animal-derived products. And as demand has increased, so have the options (and, thankfully, the quality of these products). Two of the primary drawbacks in choosing plant protein over animal protein have consistently been taste and potency. A scoop of rice protein couldn't match the protein content of whey and the grittiness and overwhelming cardboard taste of the powder was capable of ruining even the most delicious fruit combination. The answer from nutrition experts, led in particular by famed vegan athlete Brendan Brazier, was to broaden the ingredient list and take advantage of the wide array of plant proteins. The result: Instead of finding a ton of "soy protein" or "sprouted brown rice protein" on the shelves, you'll see packages of "plant protein" that mix combinations of protein from pea shoots, brown rice, chia seeds, hemp seeds, alfalfa sprouts and more. The result has been smoother-tasting supplements that can pack up to 25 grams of protein per serving.

SOY PROTEIN SUPPLEMENT

SERVING SIZE: 1 scoop (28 grams)		CALORIES: 95
CARBS: 2 grams	PROTEIN: 23 grams	FAT: 1 gram

While there have been a lot of rumors about soy raising estrogen levels or hampering testosterone, there's very little evidence to back it up. The fact remains that soy is an excellent source of plant-based protein. While it doesn't pack the same protein levels per scoop as whey or casein, soy won't give you a dose of animal-based products like other protein sources will. And, if you're a proponent of *The China Study*, you may just find soy the safer, healthier way to go.

SILKEN TOFU: AN AUTHENTIC ALTERNATIVE

Can't stand the texture of vegan protein powders? Trust us, you're not alone. If you just can't take the taste of powder supplements anymore, or if you want a break, try silken tofu instead. Roughly translated from Japanese as "soft bean curd," silken tofu is often eaten raw in Japan as everything from an appetizer to dessert. The softest varieties blend extremely well into smoothies, have little or no distinct taste, and have about 8 grams of soy protein per serving. It doesn't make for the most efficient protein source, but it can be a welcome break from powders.

MIXED-PLANT PROTEIN SUPPLEMENTS

VEGA ONE

SERVING SIZE: 1 scoop (39 grams)		CALORIES: 140
CARBS: 12 grams	PROTEIN: 15 grams	FAT: 3 grams

VEGA SPORT

SERVING SIZE: 1 scoop (39 grams)		CALORIES: 140
CARBS: 12 grams	PROTEIN: 24 grams	FAT: 3 grams

The newest mixed-plant protein supplements are the closest things to whey, casein and egg that you'll find on the market. Most of them offer a combination that includes different levels of pea, rice, chia and hemp in order to balance out and maximize the supplement as a source for complete protein. They also tend to go a lot further in supplying BCAAs (branched-chain amino acids), which are typically found mostly in animal products but comprise up to 40 percent of the amino acids in muscle tissue. While mixed-plant protein supplements still haven't quite conquered the taste and texture issues (even the newest concoctions can be gritty) when compared to animal-based products, they are truly the most comparable option if you're choosing a vegan approach to smoothie making.

RICE PROTEIN SUPPLEMENT

SERVING SIZE: 1 scoop (15 grams)	**CALORIES:** 60
CARBS: 2 grams	**PROTEIN:** 12 grams	**FAT:** 0 grams

Rice protein, specifically protein derived from sprouted brown rice, is generally considered the least problematic protein supplement of all. It is figuratively as plain and boring as, well, white rice. And for a lot of people with food sensitivities, that's a very good thing. The main drawback to rice protein is that compared to other protein sources, especially animal-based ones, rice protein is fairly inefficient. A single serving has less than half the protein of a serving of whey or egg, and the protein it does deliver is tougher for your body to process into muscle. The fact of the matter is, if you're training hard and doing a lot of damage to your muscles, rice probably isn't the answer on its own. Instead, try mixing in rice-protein shakes every so often to give your body a break from some of the more intense protein sources.

BEANS

Beans are superb energy sources that will power you throughout the day! Beans are a remarkably cheap alternative to just about any other protein source (they're the primary protein source for most civilizations around the world) and they also provide tons of cholesterol-lowering fiber and complex carbs—the kind you burn slowly throughout the day. Because of their distinct flavors, beans may sound like a weird smoothie addition, but when balanced with the right ingredients, a handful of beans adds a thick creamy texture without really changing the taste. If you're ready to give a bean-enriched smoothie a shot, the main question you'll face is, should you buy your beans dry or canned?

The biggest problem with dry beans is they need to be cooked. Uncooked beans often contain phytates, proteins that can cause digestive discomfort. This means that if you buy dry beans you are going to have to prepare them by soaking them in water and then cooking them on the stove. Still, we think the positives of dry beans outweigh the negatives. Not only do freshly cooked dry beans taste better, but they retain more nutritional value than the canned version.

WHITE BEANS

SERVING SIZE: ½ cup (90 grams)		CALORIES: 125
CARBS: 22 grams	PROTEIN: 8 grams	FAT: 0.5 gram

Any food that can keep the entire U.S. Navy going strong for the entire nineteenth century must be special, and the white, navy or cannellini bean—whatever you want to call it—did just that. These mildly flavored little guys are chock-full of protein, fiber, vitamins and minerals, and are the very best natural source of phosphatidylserine, a magical compound that can help improve athletic performance, decrease muscle damage and soreness, lower cortisol levels and improve recovery times! Unfortunately, you'd need to eat about 4 cups of white beans a day for 10 days to realize these benefits (although we think it's worth it). Some protein supplements contain phosphatidylserine derived from soybeans and white beans.

A hundred grams of cooked navy beans (a little more than half a cup) contains 140 calories, over 8 grams of protein, and nearly half your daily value of dietary fiber. Navy beans are also an excellent source of folate, thiamin, vitamin B6 and just about every mineral imaginable except sodium! Specifically, navy beans are an excellent source of manganese and a good source of calcium, iron, magnesium, phosphorous, potassium, zinc, copper and selenium. Try tossing a handful of white beans in a fruit-based smoothie—your taste buds won't notice them, but your body will.

LENTILS

SERVING SIZE: ¼ cup (about 100 grams)		CALORIES: 100
CARBS: 17 grams	PROTEIN: 8 grams	FAT: 0 grams

Unlike other dry legumes that can require overnight soaking and lengthy cooking, lentils are quick and easy to cook from scratch. And nutritionally, these little beans are healthy powerhouses. A quarter cup of lentils will provide you with 8 complete grams of protein, 17 grams of complex carbohydrates and 0 grams of fat. In addition to an excellent macronutrient score, lentils also supply about 19 percent of your daily iron needs, 45 percent of your folate and 11 percent of your daily potassium. A quarter cup of lentils will blend smoothly into any smoothie, adding a rich, creamy texture. You may notice that lentils add a slightly nutty taste, but at worst it will be a barely noticeable change.

BLACK BEANS

SERVING SIZE: ¼ cup (40 grams)		CALORIES: 57
CARBS: 10 grams	PROTEIN: 4 grams	FAT: 0.5 gram

Black beans—technically known as black turtle beans—are dense, delicious beans that provide the nutritional benefits of most beans: protein, carbs, and a slew of vitamins and minerals. One hundred grams of cooked black beans (about the maximum you'll want in a smoothie) contain almost 9 grams of protein (18 percent of your RDV), 24 grams of carbs (8 percent), and 9 grams of dietary fiber (35 percent). Black beans are also good sources of folate and thiamin, excellent sources of manganese and contain trace to moderate amounts of every other mineral except for, yep, you guessed it, sodium! Because of their carb content, black beans are a great way to start off the day or to help your body recover after a long workout. A handful of black beans is barely noticeable in chocolate smoothies and adds an interesting twist to green smoothies.

GARBANZO BEANS (CHICKPEAS)

SERVING SIZE: ½ cup (82 grams)		CALORIES: 135
CARBS: 22 grams	PROTEIN: 7 grams	FAT: 2 grams

This ancient bean—probably one of the first cultivated legumes—is a staple throughout the world (and in most U.S. grocery stores in the form of hummus). If you've ever dipped a vegetable in hummus and loved the result, then a green chickpea smoothie just might be for you. Chickpeas are super low in fat and sodium, but high in protein, carbs and dietary fiber. A hundred grams will provide you roughly with 164 calories, 9 grams of protein (18 percent of your RDV), 28 grams of carbs (9 percent) and 7.5 grams of dietary fiber (30 percent). They are also an absolutely stellar source of manganese (52 percent) and folate (43 percent), as well as containing virtually every important mineral—except for sodium! Some recent studies and examples show that a very small percentage of people have anaphylaxis when they exercise soon after eating chickpeas, so take care if you think you may be at risk of an adverse reaction.

DECADENT EXTRAS

CACAO

SERVING SIZE: 1 ounce (28 grams)		CALORIES: 168
CARBS: 13 grams	PROTEIN: 2 grams	FAT: 12 grams

Chocolate lovers rejoice! The favorite dessert of millions of people comes from the cacao bean, which is actually so healthy it's considered a superfood. Bitter and rich, the cacao bean contains a ton of antioxidants and is linked to improved cardiovascular health and decreased cancer rates.

Just one tablespoon of unsweetened, dry cacao powder is an incredible source of nutrients. With just 12 calories, a tablespoon of cacao offers 1 gram of protein, 3 grams of carbs and nearly 2 grams of dietary fiber (7 percent of your daily recommended value). It is also rich in magnesium, manganese and copper. But in addition to its nutritional content, cacao powder is an excellent addition to pretty much any smoothie because of the chocolaty taste it adds (keep in mind that it's pretty bitter, so you may want to add a natural sweetener like agave to supplement a cacao smoothie.) Cacao nibs are a nice topper to any cocoa powder–based smoothie. Be aware that cacao is full of theobromine, a caffeine-like stimulant that can keep you up, so it's best to drink cacao-laden smoothies early in the day.

SOUR CREAM (WHOLE FAT)

SERVING SIZE: ½ cup (100 grams)		CALORIES: 181
CARBS: 7 grams	PROTEIN: 7 grams	FAT: 14 grams

Sour cream in a smoothie can sound a bit unappealing, but what you may not know is that sour cream is actually a delicious "secret" ingredient to a number of commercial fruit smoothies. Not only does it add a creamy thickness, but it also adds a slightly sweet, slightly sour twist that can be very tasty. In fact, many smoothie aficionados toss a dollop of sour cream into *every smoothie they make.*

Although sour cream tends to get a rap as an unhealthy condiment, it's not bad in moderation. While 90 percent of its calories come from fat (and half of that being saturated fat), on the whole, it's actually not that caloric. A single serving is two spoonfuls and only packs about 50 calories. Furthermore, sour cream is a good source of calcium, vitamin A, vitamin B12 and phosphorous. But it's not a great source of protein (you would need an unhealthy four or five spoonfuls to get a decent amount) so use sour cream only for taste.

SEVEN

LIQUID BASES

Unless your smoothie is made primarily from a water-saturated fruit like watermelon, it's hard to make it drinkable without a liquid base. Most recipes in this book call for one to two cups of a liquid in order to give the smoothie the right consistency, but you should adjust the recipes to your own preferences. Some smoothie drinkers prefer thick, milkshake-like smoothies, using only half a cup of liquid. Others may enjoy a juice-like smoothie with a hydrating fusion of three cups of liquid. In general, how much liquid you add is going to depend on the thickness and consistency of your other ingredients. A green smoothie, for example, made entirely of fibrous, leafy greens, will require more liquid than a fruit smoothie made from juicy oranges or pineapples.

Liquid bases range drastically in terms of flavor, nutrition and consistency, with the most basic being purified water. We recommend that you start your smoothie-making journey with a water base to begin. Water allows you to isolate the fruit, green and protein ingredients and flavors so you can determine what your taste buds (and your body) prefer. Once you've established recipes you feel comfortable with, begin experimenting with more exotic bases like almond milk, coconut water or even brewed teas. Not only are the other bases more nutritious than plain water, but they provide subtle and unique flavor profiles that can take a smoothie from ordinary to extraordinary.

PURIFIED WATER

When it comes to making smoothies, no liquid base is simpler than water, an excellent choice for smoothies already packed with strong, well-balanced flavors. Furthermore, a balance of ice with any liquid base can give smoothies that refreshing coolness and slightly chunky texture. Also, many public water sources in America and increasingly throughout Europe are infused with fluoride, which helps keep your teeth strong and healthy. Keep in mind that while most public water supplies, especially those in America and industrialized countries, are heavily regulated, they still contain trace amounts of toxins and other harmful substances. Furthermore, no regulation yet exists on certain pharmaceutical drugs and perchlorate, a salt that can affect thyroid function. For these reasons, we highly suggest you filter or purify any tap water you plan on consuming.

FORTIFIED WATERS

As inexpensive and accessible as tap water is, it is not sufficient to keep the body properly hydrated during periods of intense exercise—you need electrolytes. Electrolytes are minerals, or ions, like sodium, potassium, calcium, magnesium, chloride, hydrogen phosphate and hydrogen carbonate that are essential to human function and that are shed through respiration and sweating. During exercise, electrolytes help the body direct and balance water levels, and are vital for proper nerve and muscle function. In other words, without proper electrolyte levels, your workouts are going to be a lot more difficult and less effective.

Electrolyte-fortified water is especially important for endurance athletes exercising for hours on end or for people exercising in extreme heat. While some people opt for sports drinks like Gatorade, which do often provide the appropriate electrolytes, most sports drinks are loaded with sugars, artificial dyes and other unhealthy additives. You don't need to fill your body with unnecessary junk; electrolyte-fortified water, which you can purchase in the store pre-mixed or as an add-in powder packet, is just as effective.

In addition, it's very easy to make your own electrolyte-fortified sports drink at home by following this simple recipe:

ALL-NATURAL SPORTS DRINK

2 cups water
½ cup citrus juice
1 to 4 tablespoons honey or agave
sea salt, to taste

WHOLE DAIRY MILK

SERVING SIZE: 1 cup (245 grams)		CALORIES: 146
CARBS: 13 grams	PROTEINS: 8 grams	FAT: 8 grams

Right off the bat, we strongly suggest using plant-based alternatives to animal milks in all of your smoothies. But if you want to use traditional milk in your smoothies there are plenty of benefits. Milk is excellent for muscle recovery after workouts and is absolutely chock-full of nutrition—it's very high in protein, calcium, vitamin D, riboflavin, vitamin B12 and phosphorous, and is also a good source of thiamin, vitamin B6, folate, pantothenic acid, magnesium, potassium, sodium, zinc and selenium. Still, cow milk is very problematic. Depending on which milk you choose, be aware that it may contain high amounts of saturated fat (low-fat does not), natural sugars and lactose. Even if you're not technically lactose-intolerant, you still may have some trouble digesting the lactose and/or the casein contained in milk, making it less than ideal before a hard workout. Finally, many dairy cows are raised with growth hormones and antibiotics that are potentially harmful to your health, so make sure to choose organic milk. Of course, instead of cow milk, we highly suggest easily digested alternatives such as plant-based milk substitutes or coconut water.

ALMOND MILK

SERVING SIZE: 1 cup (240 grams)		CALORIES: 30
CARBS: 1 gram	PROTEINS: 1 gram	FAT: 2–3 grams

When it comes to nut milks, almond milk is definitely the way to go. Made from finely ground almonds and water (sometimes with flavors and sweeteners added), almond milk is a tasty and nutritious milk substitute. While nut milks contain no dairy and are vegan, almond milk is almost always the least expensive and most readily available. It also is low in fat and is a good source of vitamins and minerals, making it a good liquid base for those looking to lose weight or build athletic endurance.

Specifically, a cup of almond milk contains only 30 calories, is low in carbs and contains good quantities of fiber, vitamin E, riboflavin, magnesium, manganese, phosphorous and copper. Some brands supplement the milk with calcium and vitamin D, so make sure to take a look at the nutritional data on the carton for the presence of these items. Keep in mind that almond milks contain sodium, and those with added sweeteners are often high in sugars and fats.

HOMEMADE ALMOND MILK

1 cup raw almonds (blanched or regular)

6 cups water, divided

Optional Ingredients and Sweeteners:

dash of salt

1 teaspoon vanilla extract

dash of ground cinnamon

1 to 1½ tablespoons natural sweetener (i.e., honey, agave or maple syrup)

Step 1—Choose Your Almonds: Make sure to buy unroasted almonds. Almonds can be blanched (almonds with the skin removed) or regular, but you may have to more diligently strain almonds that still have the skin.

Step 2—Soak: Soak your almonds in 2 cups of water overnight to make them softer.

Step 3—Strain and blend: Strain the water from your almonds and then toss the softened almonds in the blender with 1 cup of fresh water. Blend until you get a smooth almond puree.

Step 4 (Optional)—Flavor to taste: Add a dash of salt, sweeteners and flavors such as vanilla, cinnamon, maple syrup, honey or agave.

Step 5—Add remaining water: Add the rest of the water (3 cups) and blend!

Step 6—Strain: Pour your almond milk through a nut milk bag to remove the almond pulp to give your final product that perfectly smooth texture. Homemade almond milk will keep in the refrigerator for up to 1 week.

SOY MILK

SERVING SIZE: 1 cup (245 grams)		CALORIES: 131
CARBS: 15 grams	PROTEINS: 8 grams	FAT: 4 grams

Milk made from soybeans is among the most popular animal milk substitutes and is certainly one of the oldest, dating back nearly 2,000 years in China. Soy milk contains almost exactly the same amount of protein as cow milk, but contains almost no calcium (some store brands supplement their soy milk with calcium carbonate.)

In addition to containing about 16 percent your RDV of protein, a cup of soy milk contains 131 calories, is an excellent source of vitamin B6, magnesium, potassium and iron, and provides solid amounts of carbs, dietary fiber and calcium. Like milk, it comes in different fat proportions, such as 2 percent and 4 percent Soy milk has a moderate amount of fat, and because of the high phytic acid content, the digestive system cannot process much of its mineral content such as zinc and iron.

COCONUT MILK AND COCONUT WATER

Coconut milk and coconut water are actually independent parts of the fruit. Coconut water is the semi-transparent liquid found in the center of young coconuts. Coconut milk is a thick, creamy substance made by essentially juicing the rich coconut meat through a strainer lined with cheesecloth. And the nutritional profiles of these two liquids differ dramatically. Coconut water is extremely good for you, containing various nutrients, including calcium, vitamin C, riboflavin, manganese, potassium, magnesium, iron and phosphorous.

Coconut milk, on the other hand, is loaded with saturated fat, so you should enjoy it in moderation. Still, coconut milk is a rich and decadent ingredient that can be a wonderful once-in-a-while ingredient for fun, creamy smoothies while adding a rich blend of minerals, especially manganese, and to a lesser extent copper, selenium, iron, phosphorous and potassium. To save on fat calories, you can also use light coconut milk, which provides tropical flavor but fewer grams of fat. (For more information, see "Coconut" on page 59.)

TEAS

It may be a bit of a surprise, but what we think of as the wide variety of traditional "tea" (green, black, white, etc.) are all derived from the leaves of the same plant, *Camellia sinensis*. Black tea, green tea, white tea and oolong are all made using tea leaves that are processed differently as the leaves are dried. While green and black are the most popular tea flavors on their own, green tea is the most common liquid base for smoothies, as it has a mild, delicate flavor, more antioxidants and less caffeine than black tea. Green tea is also extremely good for you. It has a high concentration of catechins, antioxidants that are shown to have extensive well-being benefits like preventing inflammation and reducing muscular pain. In addition, the presence of caffeine (which stimulates) and the amino acid theanine (which calms and eases stress) can produce a calm alertness, especially when consumed in the morning. All teas from the tea plant protect against heart disease and cancers of the mouth, esophegus, prostate, pancreas, liver, colon, breast, skin and lungs.

Tea can also refer to herbal teas made from fruit and herbal blends, and many provide nutritional and emotional benefits beyond traditional tea. Rose hip, for example, contains a high dose of vitamin C and lycopene, a powerful antioxidant. South African rooibos also contains antioxidants such as phenolic compounds. It may help with allergies, blood circulation and digestion. And of course, chamomile contains essential oils and other ingredients that soothe the stomach and can help you fall asleep—making it a perfect liquid base for a bedtime smoothie.

SECTION III

SMOOTHIE-BASED DIETS: USING SMOOTHIES TO LOSE WEIGHT OR GAIN MUSCLE

Smoothies are incredibly versatile tools if you're looking to make changes to your physique—regardless of whether you are looking to lose weight or gain muscle. Because each and every smoothie recipe can be catered to deliver your body a range of micro and macronutrients, you can tweak your daily recipes to fit into carefully crafted calorie-intake goals. If you're looking to lose weight, you simply should be consuming fewer calories than you exert during the day. If you're looking to gain weight in the form of muscle mass, you're task is a bit more complicated—in addition to increasing your daily caloric intake, you'll also need to focus on "nutrient timing," delivering your body the carbs, fats and proteins it needs at the correct periods of the day according to your schedule of activities. But regardless of your aim, simple-to-make and easy-to-drink smoothies will make your goals much more manageable.

EIGHT

LOSING WEIGHT WITH SMOOTHIES

If your goal is to shed pounds quickly, smoothies can be a godsend. Unlike traditional calorie-restriction diets that essentially starve off the pounds, a diet based around healthy green smoothies allows you to fully nourish your body, with a proper balance of macronutrients, vitamins and minerals, while keeping your daily caloric intake low enough to begin losing weight. The best part about a smoothie-based weight loss diet is that there is nothing *fad* about it. By consuming a balanced amount of protein, carbohydrates and healthy fat, you won't end up bouncing from one weight to another and you won't experience the negative emotional, physical and physiological side effects of some of the more draconian diet plans out there. In fact, many people that we've spoken to have said that after a couple weeks of trying a smoothie-based diet, they were able to make smoothies a permanent part of their diet and have remained healthy and fit ever since.

CHOOSE YOUR GOALS

Losing weight through calorie restriction requires a custom approach based on factors such as your body type, metabolism rate, muscle mass, age, current weight and average daily exercise. Losing weight quickly on this diet is all about burning more calories in your everyday activities than you consume.

The average (sedentary) adult needs to consume 2,000–2,500 calories per day (with no additional exercise) in order to replenish the stored calories that are naturally burned off from everyday activities like breathing, thinking, sleeping and eating. If you exercise daily, you may end up burning 2,500–3,000 calories during the day.

Losing weight means creating a **calorie deficit** for your body—denying it enough calories to replenish those burned calories and forcing your body to turn to its natural fat reserves to power you physically.

CALCULATING A POUND OF FAT

The common calculation used by dieters is that a pound of body fat is equal to approximately 3,500 calories. Meaning that you would need to create a 3,500-calorie deficit to shed that extra pound of fat. In reality, the equation is not quite that easy. A pound of body fat is not uniform in its lipid makeup, and the ability to process and metabolize fat for energy use can differ from person to person.

Instead of abiding by a strict single number, you should estimate your own fat-burning potential by placing yourself on a sliding scale based on your own experience. On one end, individuals with faster metabolisms can expect a pound of fat to be equal to approximately 2,750 calories. If you find burning off body fat to be a bit more difficult, you should calculate your average pound of body fat to contain about 3,750 calories. That 1,000 calorie difference can seem like a big discrepancy, but properly estimating your body's potential can make all the difference when it comes to achieving your weight loss goals.

ESTIMATING A CALORIE DEFICIT TO HELP ACHIEVE FAT LOSS

Now that you have a better estimate of how efficiently your body can burn fat, it's time to figure out your goals and come up with a game plan.

Let's say that you are a 5'9", 35-year-old man who weighs 175 pounds and exercises about three times per week. Over the past few years you've noticed that burning off that extra winter weight has been tougher than when you were younger. Based on your daily habits, you should expect to burn an average of 2,350 calories per day. And based on your place on the fat-calorie content scale, you should expect a pound of your body fat to contain around 3,200 calories.

Creating a calorie restriction plan from that is pretty simple. Take your calculated average calorie burn (2,350 calories), chose a reasonable calorie-intake goal (1,600 calories) and you'll achieve a daily calorie deficit of 750 calories. Based on your estimate of how many calories are in a pound of your body fat (3,200) sticking to a restrictive diet will help you burn a pound of fat of your body in just four to five days (3,200/750 = 4.27 days).

If you're interested in calculating your own estimated daily calorie burn, you can find an excellent calorie calculator at www.mayoclinic.org, or by searching for "calorie calculator" online.

PLANNING YOUR DIET

Once you have your weight-loss goal set, you should calculate the length of the diet you'll need to embark upon in order to accomplish it. For example, if you take our sample 175-pound man from the previous section and give him a goal of trimming down from 175 pounds to 170 pounds, he will need to stick to his calorie-restricting diet for 20–25 days to shed the weight. Depending on your weight-loss goals, you should plan to stick with your diet from anywhere from a quick three days to a full month.

The most effective way to lose weight and keep it off is to get regular exercise and follow a balanced diet rich in all your necessary macronutrients (protein, fat and carbs) without restricting your calorie intake to the point that the diet becomes difficult to follow. Therefore, we suggest choosing a realistic calorie restriction target depending on your weight and gender that lands somewhere between 1,200 and 1,600 calories per day.

EAT THOSE FATS TO LOSE THAT FAT!

When you're preparing your daily diet smoothies, remember to include ingredients like chia seeds, almonds, walnuts and avocado. The healthy monounsaturated fats in these ingredients may increase your caloric intake, but in the long run they'll actually help you lose weight faster by keeping your body functioning properly. Good fats can prevent the development of fat around your belly, help boost your metabolism and absorb vital nutrients like vitamins A, D and E.

PLANNING A CALORIE-RESTRICTIVE MENU

From our experience, the easiest way to achieve a calorie-restrictive diet with smoothies is to use your blended drinks as meal replacements. Because smoothies can be made with a healthy balance of macronutrients, they will allow you to feel full, properly nourished and energetic, despite their low calorie content. In the recipe section of this book, your best selection for low-calorie meal replacements can be found in "20 under 200: Fat-Busting Smoothies" (page 151). Use these recipes, or experiments of your own, to build healthy, enjoyable smoothies that can stand in for your normal lunches or dinners.

Begin your diet by swapping out one of your main daily meals (either lunch or dinner) with a smoothie. Pay attention to how your body feels afterward and how it affects your following meal. Are you still hungry? By the time your next meal rolls around (either dinner or breakfast) do you find yourself eating more food or eating more quickly? If the answer is "yes" to either of those questions, there are simple adjustments you can make to ensure you stick to your diet plan.

The most effective change is to break your smoothie meal into two separate mini-meals spaced about two hours apart. For example, try drinking a smoothie (from "20 under 200: Fat-Busting Smoothies," page 151) at 12 p.m. and then another at 2 p.m. Spacing out your calorie intake will allow your body to better metabolize the macronutrients for energy use and will leave you feeling more sated as you approach dinner, preventing you from potentially overeating.

After a week with a one-meal smoothie substitution, try introducing another recipe into your daily routine. If you tend to eat quick breakfasts that contain sugar, swap it out for a robust, nutrient-rich smoothie. Or, if you have a sweet tooth, try swapping out that after-meal dessert with a small all-fruit smoothie.

Within a couple of weeks of daily smoothie consumption, you'll begin to see significant changes in your energy level, dietary habits and overall well-being. Many people experience a profound dietary shift, where the benefits their fruit- and vegetable-rich smoothie meals leave them feeling better and more rewarded than heavy lunches or dinners—inspiring them to add more and more smoothies to their daily menus.

Once you're fully comfortable with using smoothies to help lose weight, we suggest structuring your daily meals around the following sample menus.

OPTION A: LUNCH SMOOTHIE SUBSTITUTIONS

	FOOD	TOTAL CALORIES
Breakfast	Green smoothie + breakfast food	400–600
Early Lunch	Green smoothie	200
Late Lunch	Green smoothie	200
Dinner	Your choice	400–600
Dessert	Fruit smoothie	50
Totals		1,250–1,650

OPTION B: DINNER SMOOTHIE SUBSTITUTIONS

	FOOD	TOTAL CALORIES
Breakfast	Green smoothie + breakfast food	400–600
Lunch	Your choice	400–600
Early Dinner	Green smoothie	200
Late Dinner	Green smoothie	200
Dessert	Fruit smoothie	50
Totals		1,250–1,650

BREAKFAST: THE MOST IMPORTANT MEAL OF THE DAY

The one golden rule in starting your day off healthy is *never skip breakfast*. This is especially true if you are trying to lose weight. A well-balanced breakfast that contains carbs, proteins and fat can help boost your metabolism dramatically for the duration of the day and it will keep you from over-indulging on midmorning snacks. Skipping breakfast can actually shock your body into mini-survival mode, slowing your metabolism in order to store up calories. Eating a large breakfast may sound counterintuitive for weight loss, but in the research project behind Dr. Daniela Jakubowicz's *The Big Breakfast Diet,* patients who consumed a well-balanced breakfast consisting of 600 or more calories lost over 15 percent more body fat than patients consuming limited-calorie breakfasts under 300 calories.

That being said, Americans tend to consume a *lot* of calories at breakfast. A bowl of Starbucks' oatmeal can pack as many as 25 grams of fat; an Egg McMuffin has 300 calories. Even a single slice of bacon comes with 41 calories. And that's before adding in drinks like lattes (120-210 calories) and cappuccinos (up to 120 calories). Without realizing it, you can consume a quick 800 empty calories before 10 a.m.

Green smoothies allow you to carefully control your calorie intake while getting all of the vital nutrients necessary to thrive through the day.

If you are trying to lose weight, you should start your day with a full 400-600 calories, which can either be consumed with a combination of a traditional breakfast items (like a bowl of oatmeal) and a smoothie or just a hearty smoothie alone. It all depends on your preference and what will make you feel the best as you start your day.

In the "Morning Smoothies" chapter (page 145) we offer some blends that are tailor-made to offer you a healthy balance of all the macronutrients (carbs, protein and fat) as well as a full infusion of micronutrients from greens and fruits that will boost your energy and alertness levels.

SPLITTING ONE MEAL A DAY

Because we live busy lives and you're not always going to find yourself near your blender and produce supply, this diet allows for interchangeable lunches and dinners. If you have an important lunch meeting with a client, go for it! Feel free to order that club sandwich or turkey burger. You can always replace tonight's dinner with fresh, healthy green smoothies and get all the benefits. And the same is true for fun dinner dates or parties; you don't have to feel like you're a slave to your green smoothies. Simply plan ahead by doubling up on green drinks for breakfast and lunch, and then have a great time at dinner.

If you've ever tried skimping on your calorie intake during lunch, you've probably had to face the consequences later in the afternoon or evening. By the time dinner rolls around, you're ready to eat a cow. And unfortunately, that is often what ends up happening—a light lunch turns into a very heavy dinner.

To combat that tendency, we have found it remarkably effective to split the smoothie meal of the day into two—an early lunch or dinner (about an hour before you would normally eat lunch or dinner) and a late lunch or dinner (about two hours *after* you'd normally eat lunch or an hour after you'd normally eat dinner). Splitting your second green smoothie meal into two allows you to keep your second-meal calorie consumption under 300 calories (total) and has a tremendous impact on how much you end up consuming during your final, normal meal.

PRE-BED DESSERT SMOOTHIES

A light, simple pre-bedtime or dessert smoothie can do wonders for helping you shed pounds during your diet. That's because when you sleep, your metabolism tends to hit its slowest pace and relies on fat and protein stores to power your vital functions while you slumber. A small, protein-heavy smoothie can help keep your metabolism working overtime while protecting your muscles from being robbed of vital protein. In addition to keeping your metabolism's pace raised, the smoothie will prevent you from feeling hungry in the middle of the night as well as overeating the next day.

You don't want to overdo this after-dinner or late-night smoothie; stick to simple ingredients that don't have a lot of sugar—like a smoothie made from strawberries, Greek yogurt and unsweetened almond milk. It'll be enough to satisfy your sweet tooth while providing at least 5-10 grams of protein.

For a full list of pre-bed, light-calorie smoothie recipes, see the "Evening Smoothies" chapter (page 196).

NINE

PACKING ON MUSCLE MASS WITH SMOOTHIES

Athletes looking to pack on muscle mass rapidly, or to maintain muscle mass, need to consume a lot of calories. Where the average adult may require about 2,000 calories every day just to maintain a healthy body, and an active athlete, like someone who runs more than a mile a day, spends an hour in the gym daily or regularly attends yoga or fitness classes, can require up to 3,000 calories, bodybuilders and strength-training athletes in the process of building muscle mass may need up to 4,000 calories each and every day during training to properly feed the body and muscles. And if you've ever tried consuming that many calories in a day you know that it can be an exhausting task and can feel as though all you are doing is shoveling food into your mouth.

A high-calorie, high-protein smoothie program takes an enormous amount of the stress of constantly having to eat out of the equation. The diet we've designed here allows you to consume half your daily calories in easy-to-make, easy-to-drink smoothies, leaving you with a normal daily diet to enjoy. As an added benefit, not only does a smoothie-rich, calorie-heavy diet make the process of gaining muscle mass less of a chore, but it allows you to efficiently and effectively consume between 10 and 15 full servings of fruit and vegetables every day—making it one of the healthiest possible ways to gain muscle mass.

UNDERSTANDING YOUR BODY'S NEEDS

We've already discussed a bit about the different roles the three big macronutrients—protein, carbohydrates and fats—play in overall health (see "Nourish the Body," page 16), but let's get a little more specific. Finding the perfect balance between protein, carbs and fats is essential for growing strong, beautiful muscles. Remember, even though proteins directly feed your muscles, you won't have the energy to work out without carbohydrates and fats.

Carbohydrates are vital for muscle function. Your digestive system breaks down carbs into simpler sugars for absorption into the bloodstream. Once absorbed, these sugars can be taken to your liver and muscles to be stored as glycogen. It is the glycogen stored within your muscles that is particularly important for generating the energy needed to sustain high-intensity exercise. Because glycogen is so readily accessible, it is the most common energy reserve utilized by your muscles during intense exercises such as wind sprints or strength training. It is also burned during the initial minutes of any exercise.

The body also needs fats, which provide the highest concentration of energy (1 gram of fat provides about 9 calories, compared to 4 each for carbs and protein). While fats help the body synthesize and burn glycogen during short, powerful workouts, fats are the body's preferred fuel source during longer, steadier exercises such as jogging, swimming or cycling. Keep in mind that your body turns fat into a usable source of energy slowly (as long as five to six hours after eating), so in order to have newly metabolized fat ready to fuel an activity, you should time your consumption of fat-containing foods early. And while everybody knows that too much fat can lead to health issues such as obesity, diabetes and heart problems, it's important to know that the opposite, while rare, is also true: If you don't have enough fat reserves during a sustained workout, your body will utilize the next best energy source— your muscles.

Below we've outlined the macronutrient balance for three potential dietary days for a common athlete. The first day, "Aerobic Day," would be your typical day involving a 30 to 60 minute aerobic exercise like a long run, spin, sporting game or fitness class. The second day, "Anaerobic Day," is focused on anaerobic exercise, your weight-training day where you are focused on building muscle. The third day, "Off Day," is what you should consume on your training-free day, where exercise is limited to basic daily functions like walking.

Keep in mind that all of these numbers should be adjusted to your personal needs and individual body type. You should take into account how fast your metabolism processes food (the faster your metabolism, the more calories you'll need), how big you are and how old you are. And keep in mind that the body is *always* burning calories, even in your sleep (the average person burns about 500 calories sleeping), so make sure you are consuming what you need to thrive every day.

In order to calculate your daily macronutrient intake, you should set basic caloric-intake goals before you begin your day. For example, on your off day you may want to shoot for a 2,000-calorie day, but a day that includes a 10k run may need to be bumped up to 3,000 calories. If you are looking to put on several pounds of muscle, your body may require up to 4,000 calories during every 24-hour period, depending on your body size and gender.

In order to properly balance your macronutrient intake (carbs, protein and fat) for optimal performance, you should calculate out your caloric intake in grams. Here is a simple calculation for each:

1 gram carbs = 4 calories

1 gram protein = 4 calories

1 gram fat = 9 calories

Therefore, if you consume 80 grams of protein, 500 grams of carbs and 75 grams of fat, you'll end up consuming about 3,000 calories, about enough to properly power the body and build muscle during a day containing a high-intensity workout. Again, you'll want to balance your intake to your specific needs.

	AEROBIC TRAINING DAY	ANAEROBIC (WEIGHT TRAINING) DAY	OFF DAY
Carb requirement	Men 400–500 grams	Men 350–500 grams	Men 250–350 grams
	Women 300–400 grams	Women 250–350 grams	Women 200–300 grams
Protein requirement	Men 80 grams	Men 110 grams	Men 55 grams
	Women 65 grams	Women 90 grams	Women 45 grams
Fat requirement	Men 75 grams	Men 70 grams	Men 60 grams
	Women 65 grams	Women 60 grams	Women 50 grams

The right balance of protein, carbs and fats depends on a number of factors, including what your body looks like now, what you want your body to look like in the future, your metabolism, your workout plan and your overall activity level. Whatever your goals are, it is vital to develop a menu that balances all three macronutrients. Focus less on maintaining rigid protein-to-carb-to-fat ratios and more on where you are getting your calories. If you are getting most of your calories from healthy, whole food sources like fruits, vegetables, nuts, other plant products like unsweetened soy milk or nut butters, and lean meats and omega-3-rich fish, chances are you'll be healthy, happy and full of energy.

Of course, smoothies are a fun, delicious way of making sure you get the right balance of macronutrients (not to mention micronutrients like vitamins and minerals). Not only can they help fuel you during a workout and help your muscles recover after exercise, but enjoying a smoothie as a snack or pre-meal treat can help ensure you're filled up on nutritious natural foods rather than high-fat meats and processed foods.

USING SMOOTHIES TO MAINTAIN MUSCLE MASS WITHOUT ADDING WEIGHT

If you're looking to maximize your physical stamina and strength, without necessarily changing your body's physical structure, you'll want to alter your smoothie plan to fit your needs. If done right, you'll be able to add a bit of lean muscle mass without adding performance-hindering weight. The trick is to use protein-rich fruit and green smoothies in addition to your current diet, which should total about 2,200–2,400 calories per day for women and 2,800–3,200 calories per day for men, and around 85 grams of protein. Of course, your caloric intake should be adjusted to your particular age, weight and daily activity level.

BALANCING YOUR PROTEIN SOURCES

Over the last several years, protein has earned a troubling reputation when it comes to long-term health. In early 2014, a University of Southern California medical study showed that a long-term, protein-heavy diet may actually be as harmful to the body as smoking more than a pack of cigarettes *a day*. Other long-term research, like that found in *The China Study*, indicates similar health concerns. Though a consensus on how much protein is too much has not been reached, what is clear is that while meats and dairy may offer you the most efficient source of protein gram for gram, a truly healthy diet will derive a large amount of proteins from plants rather than potentially cancer-causing animal protein sources.

These findings can cause a serious dilemma for health-conscious athletes in the middle of strength training. Animal-derived protein and protein supplements are hard to match in efficacy when it comes to replacing them with plant-based alternatives. While great strides have been made in the last several years with the development and release of new mixed-plant protein supplements like Vega Sport, the decision on where your protein is coming from should be a personal one. Therefore, we've included an "all-of-the-above" approach to this book, where you'll find recipes and information for both plant-based and animal-derived protein sources.

ONLY ONE SERVING OF PROTEIN POWDER A DAY

Consumer research has shown that multiple doses of packaged protein powders, such as whey, soy and casein-isolate can have adverse health effects; exposing the body to heavy metals like mercury and cadmium and excess protein consumption can put a lot of strain on your kidneys. Unlike other bodybuilding diets, a program based on natural green smoothies where you are getting protein from a wide range of sources like beans, greens and nuts will allow you to reduce your reliance on processed supplements.

NUTRIENT TIMING

One of the most important aspects of eating for muscle gain is nutrient timing. To understand nutrient timing, it's important to know your body's limitations and basic functionings. Below are the five most important rules for nutrient timing regimens to build muscle:

1. Consume at least 100 grams of protein, from varied sources, a day during weight training. Efficient muscle recovery and growth requires ample protein sources. In addition to supplements, you should try to get as much protein as possible from plants and, if it's in your diet, lean healthy meat like chicken and fish.

2. Spread out your protein consumption throughout the day. Your body can only absorb and metabolize a maximum of around 30 grams of protein at any given time. That's about the amount of protein you will get in a single smoothie with a protein supplement in it (or in about 4 ounces of cooked meat). Give yourself at least three hours between protein-heavy meals or snacks to make sure your body has ample time to use the protein it already has to work with.

3. Load up on energy before your workout. Your pre-workout smoothie (or snack) should have a ratio of 5 grams of carbs to every 1.5 grams of protein and 1 gram of fat. Within an hour of your workout, you should try to consume 20–30 grams of carbohydrates. During workouts, your body will primarily use carbs and fat as fuel, so it's best to save high-protein snacks and smoothies for after your workout.

4. Immediately after a workout, your body needs carbs and fat, as well as protein. Don't just rely on a protein shake to help you recover. Your body is still going to be burning calories in the form of carbohydrates and fat, and a balanced smoothie will allow you to maintain your energy levels while aiding in recovery.

5. Don't let your body starve at night. A bedtime protein-heavy smoothie is an absolute must if you are looking to put on muscle mass. Muscle recovery takes a long time after a workout and your muscles do a lot of efficient rebuilding overnight while you're sleeping, so make sure there are ample stores of protein available before you doze off for the night.

DAILY MEAL PLANS FOR STRENGTH-TRAINING ATHLETES

With all this information in mind, it's time to build your ideal daily smoothie plan. In order to hit a 4,000 calorie goal (with 2,000 calories coming from smoothies), you should plan a daily smoothie menu around your meals like this:

SMOOTHIE SCHEDULE FOR A 4,000 CALORIE DAILY DIET

	FOOD	TOTAL CALORIES
Breakfast	Green smoothie	500+
Mid-Morning Smoothie	Green smoothie	300
Pre-Workout Smoothie	Green smoothie	400
Recovery Smoothie	Green smoothie with protein	500
Bedtime Smoothie	Fruit smoothie	300
Total Calories		2,000

BREAKFAST SMOOTHIE

Your muscle-maximizing breakfast smoothie is designed to give you a balanced infusion of carbs, proteins and fats first thing in the morning, an ideal combination for feeding muscles that have essentially been going hungry overnight and for helping to jump-start your metabolism. None of the breakfast smoothies we recommend contain refined protein powders; you'll want to wait to use any supplements, whether animal-derived or plant-based, until after your daily workout. For breakfast smoothie recipes, we have provided ample options, including "Morning Smoothies" on page 145 (smoothies with natural additives that promote alertness) as well as calorie-rich smoothies in the "15 over 500: Calorie-Dense Smoothies" on page 187).

MID-MORNING SMOOTHIE

Your morning smoothie should be quick, simple and balanced. You only need about 300 calories at this point in the day (assuming you don't have a pre-lunch workout scheduled). In this smoothie, try to derive all of your macronutrients from plant sources only. Use seeds (like chia and flax), nuts (like almonds) and legumes (like peanuts or beans) as sources of protein and healthy fats. In addition, nutrient-rich greens like kale can be an excellent source of carbohydrates and even pack some additional complete proteins. Fill out your smoothie with a good source of carbs like berries, stone fruits or tropical treats. Remember that you're just trying to keep the body fed and energized between that big breakfast and your upcoming lunch.

PRE-WORKOUT SMOOTHIE

One of the most common mistakes we hear that people make when trying to add muscle mass is that they consume their protein-heavy smoothies *before* their aerobic or anaerobic workouts. Protein is not an ideal energy source during a workout—your body needs carbohydrates and healthy fats to power through, and if you eat a bunch of protein beforehand, you'll just end up burning off what you wanted to help rebuild your muscles with after. Instead, your pre-workout smoothies should consist primarily of carbs and lean, plant-derived fats, your top-two workout energy sources.

The primary reason to balance your intake of these two macronutrients is that, like a hybrid vehicle, your body automatically alternates between fuel sources depending on the intensity of your workout. Lower-intensity workouts, like a day of easy weights, jogging or relaxed bike riding are fueled primarily by fats. High-intensity workouts like running, team sports and even intense interval weight training tends to burn more carbs. Therefore, a healthy, balanced intake of nutrients before exercising will ensure your body is properly stocked with the right energy sources.

The smoothie recipes we've provided for carb loading on page 159 are excellent pre-workout energy boosters that we've tested over the past several years. In addition to having idea nutritional balance, the smoothies have been engineered to be as light and easy to digest as possible; you'll feel comfortable regardless of how intense your workout is. If your workout consists primarily of weight training, you should try to consume your smoothie an hour before you begin. This will give your body the optimal amount of time to absorb the macronutrients and turn them into energy. If your workout consists primarily of intense aerobic training, like a long run or spin class, you should drink your smoothie a little earlier, about an hour and a half before you start to ensure that no cramping occurs.

POST-WORKOUT SMOOTHIE

You've just had a great, exhausting workout (fueled by a balanced pre-workout smoothie). It's time to recover! You need to feed your body after a hard workout or lose the benefits all together. And the best recovery food gives your body a well-balanced infusion of every macronutrient, with an emphasis on protein of course. The reason that you don't want to focus only on consuming protein after a workout is that, even if you're mentally finished burning calories, your body isn't. After an intense workout, your body continues to burn calories at a higher rate for several hours as it slowly returns to normal. That means that you need to continue to feed it the same balance of carbs and fats that you did when you fueled it up before your workout began. That way, you won't burn off the valuable protein you're hoping to direct to repairing and building up your muscles. In addition to protein, you also need to replace the carbohydrates that have been spent, in the form of your muscles' glycogen stores, so that you'll be ready to go for your next workout. What should you drink?

PB&J: THE KING OF RECOVERY

One of the best recovery foods you can make yourself is a peanut butter and jelly sandwich (made with whole-grain bread, fresh jam and organic no-sugar-added peanut butter). It's cheap, easy to make, fairly easy to consume (it won't destroy your appetite) and you can bring it with you for quick recovery. And the nutritional makeup is exactly what your body wants. The bread and jelly supply your body with carbs and dietary fiber, and an ounce of peanut butter gives you 7–10 grams of nearly complete protein and 12–14 grams of monounsaturated and polyunsaturated fats. It's hard to beat.

When it came to crafting highly effective post-workout recovery smoothies, we took the PB&J as inspiration. We wanted to make recipes that were healthy, balanced, easy to make, portable and, above all, easy to drink every day.

BEDTIME SMOOTHIE

When you're trying to gain muscle mass, it's hard to take any time off; and consuming calories can start to feel like a job unto itself. The fact is that you need to keep feeding your muscles. It's pretty astounding actually—each pound of muscle that you add will consume about 35-40 calories every day, and that's just at rest. Put on an additional 10 pounds of muscle and you're looking at an additional burn of 350-400 calories without ever moving a muscle. And during an eight-hour night's sleep, that 10 pounds of new muscle can burn up to 135 calories on its own! With that in mind, it's no wonder that you need to consume 4,000 calories a day to keep building healthy muscle.

A key time for the consumption of a few extra protein-based calories is just before heading off to bed. During periods of extended rest, the body moves toward what is called a catabolic state—the body is actively breaking down muscle molecules before rebuilding them using these smaller building blocks to then repair them. The fuel that helps the process along is protein.

The problem is that while your body is using protein to repair muscle while you sleep, it's also burning fat and protein for basic bodily functions while you're unconscious (like breathing and staying warm). The competition over protein reserves during this overnight fast can mean muscle tissue is not getting enough protein to fully rebuild, greatly reducing the efficacy of the day's workout. In order to make sure you're getting the most amount of benefit from this evening's workout, you need ample stores of protein all night long. Not only that, but consuming a high-protein shake before bed has been shown to help burn fat since it keeps your body's metabolism from slowing down.

Slow-absorption protein sources, like casein, tend to make the most effective pre-bed smoothie bases. In your stomach, casein forms a gelatinous clump that is then slowly digested, making it sort of a time-release protein pill, feeding your body a continuous source of protein for about seven hours and helping you bridge the gap between when you go to bed and when you have the chance to eat breakfast. We've supplied several casein-heavy bedtime recipes (page 196) that will help you feed your muscles without keeping you up.

SECTION IV

SMOOTHIE RECIPES

MAKING YOUR SMOOTHIES

PREP YOUR INGREDIENTS

Always wash your fruits and vegetables before adding them to your smoothie recipe. Even "triple pre-washed" bags of greens can carry pathogens or pesticides, and those are the last things you want entering your system. Always remember that smoothies are part of a *raw diet,* and you need to take extra care in protecting your digestive system when you're not cooking your ingredients.

BLEND AWAY

Once you've washed all your fruits and vegetables, cut them into easy-to-blend pieces (up to one-inch cubes for fruits and three-inch square veggie leaves) and drop them into your blender. We like to layer the fruits and vegetables (fruit-veggie-fruit-veggie) to ensure a smooth blending process. If you're adding in supplements, seeds or nuts, place them on top of the fruits and vegetables; this will ensure they don't end up trapped below the blender blades. Once all your solid ingredients are in the blender, add your liquid base and blend at high speed until you get a consistency and texture that is pleasing to your palate. Remember that if you're using high-fiber vegetables, like collard greens, it can take a minute or so to break down the leaves into a drinkable solution.

ONE SERVING PER RECIPE

The recipes that follow have all been designed as single-serving drinks. The nutrient counts associated with each recipe are for one person, so if you'd like to make blends for more than one, you should take that into consideration if you're counting your macronutrient intake. Each smoothie in the recipe section is designed to produce a drink that is 12-20 ounces, although the quantity can vary depending on how much extra water or ice you prefer in your smoothies.

CUSTOMIZE TO YOUR TASTE

Each recipe in this collection is designed to create a palatable smoothie with a pleasing texture. But everyone has their own tastes and expectations. If your smoothie ends up too thick for your liking, you should feel free to add extra water or another liquid base to thin it out. If the result of your blend is too warm (around room temperature) for your taste, feel free to add ice to any smoothie. If you're using frozen fruits and vegetables, a bit of warm water in the blender can reduce the slushy texture. Experiment with what makes you happiest. Remember, the goal is to create a nutrient-packed drink that you'll actually enjoy.

SAVE FOR LATER

You can always save your smoothies to drink later. If you're planning on making a smoothie this morning and drinking it tonight, simply refrigerate your pre-made smoothie. Remember that by the time you are ready to drink it, the blended ingredients may have separated based on their density. Normally you can stir the smoothie back into shape using a spoon, but you can always toss a pre-made smoothie back into the blender for a couple of seconds. For smoothies that you're planning on keeping overnight or longer, you should feel free to freeze your blended smoothie in order to keep it fresh and nutritious.

TEN

MORNING SMOOTHIES

Skip the coffee and try a tailor-made morning smoothie. These recipes blend ingredients that help hydrate the body, replace nutrients lost during sleep and are rich in cognition-boosting fruits like blueberries, which have been proven to increase memory function and alertness. In addition, these smoothies have all the protein, complex carbs and healthy fats to help power the body through the morning, whether it includes a trip to the gym or just to work. Yet we understand that skipping your morning coffee is easier said than done. If that sounds impossible, try some delicious, ice-cold, coffee-based smoothies for that extra morning boost. Also, take a look at some of our anti-inflammatory smoothies, as several of the tea-based ones also make great morning pick-me-ups.

ALMOND UP

CALORIES: 266	CARBS: 43 grams
PROTEINS: 6 grams	FATS: 9.5 grams

1 cup hulled strawberries

1 banana

⅛ cup blanched raw almonds

1 cup almond milk

½ cup chilled green tea

ice, to taste

CHOWCHILLA COOLER

CALORIES: 273	CARBS: 51 grams
PROTEINS: 6.5 grams	FATS: 7 grams

½ cup hulled strawberries

1 cup coarsely chopped kale

1 banana

2 tablespoons coconut milk

1 cup coconut water

water, to taste

FLORIDA SUNRISE

CALORIES: 460	CARBS: 76 grams
PROTEINS: 20.5 grams	FATS: 11 grams

1 cup chopped mango

½ cup blueberries

2 medium oranges, peeled

1 cup whole-milk Greek yogurt

1 cup coconut water

4 ice cubes

BANANA BREAD

CALORIES: 602	CARBS: 79 grams
PROTEINS: 13.5 grams	FATS: 28.5 grams

1 banana

1 cup chopped mango

¼ cup raw walnuts (optionally soaked for up to 8 hours)

¼ cup whole-milk Greek yogurt

1 teaspoon maple syrup (optional)

2 tablespoons ground flaxseed

pinch of ground cinnamon

1 cup almond milk

BERRY MORNING PIE

CALORIES: 365	**CARBS:** 58 grams
PROTEINS: 16.5 grams	**FATS:** 9.5 grams

½ cup blueberries

½ cup blackberries

½ cup raspberries

¼ cup rolled oats, raw or cooked

¼ cup whole-milk Greek yogurt

1 cup soy milk

ESPRESSO BANANA BLAST

CALORIES: 532	**CARBS:** 88.5 grams
PROTEINS: 9.5 grams	**FATS:** 16.5 grams

2 bananas

2 shots espresso (room temperature or chilled)

¼ cup whole-milk Greek yogurt

1 ounce dark chocolate

1 cup almond milk

½ cup spinach

1 tablespoon honey (optional)

ice, to taste

MOCHA MORNING

CALORIES: 483	CARBS: 50 grams
PROTEINS: 9 grams	FATS: 28 grams

½ banana

½ avocado, peeled and pitted

1 ounce dark chocolate

¼ cup whole-milk Greek yogurt

ground cinnamon, to taste

1 tablespoon maple syrup (optional)

1½ cups brewed coffee, cooled to room temperature
    or chilled

ice, to taste

Optional addition: This smoothie works well with chocolate protein powders.

ESPRESS' YOURSELF

CALORIES: 343	CARBS: 35 grams
PROTEINS: 6 grams	FATS: 20.5 grams

1 banana

2 tablespoons natural almond butter

1 cup almond milk

2 shots espresso, room temperature or chilled

ice, to taste

Optional addition: This smoothie works well with chocolate protein powders.

APPLE & CINNAMON OATMEAL DELIGHT

CALORIES: 498	**CARBS:** 94 grams
PROTEINS: 17 grams	**FATS:** 9 grams

1 apple

1 banana

½ cup rolled oats, raw or cooked

½ cup whole-milk Greek yogurt

pinch of ground cinnamon

pinch of brown sugar

1 cup soy milk

ice, to taste

SUNDAY MORNING GINGER SNAP

CALORIES: 320	**CARBS:** 38 grams
PROTEINS: 13 grams	**FATS:** 13.5 grams

1 chopped pear

¼ cup rolled oats, raw or cooked

¼ cup whole-milk Greek yogurt

⅛ cup blanched raw almonds

1 teaspoon peeled, minced fresh ginger

1 cup almond milk

water, to taste

ELEVEN

20 UNDER 200: FAT-BUSTING SMOOTHIES

If your primary intention is weight loss, this collection of 20 smoothies, each under 200 calories, offers filling, nutrient-rich recipes. You'll still feel energized, awake and nourished after drinking them, but they won't jack up your calorie count for the day, making them excellent meal substitutions if you're restricting calories. In addition to nutrients, these smoothies are also packed with rich amounts of dietary fiber, which will help regulate your digestion, keep you feeling full and clean out your system.

To cut down on fat- or carb-heavy foods and snacks, have a glass of one of these smoothies whenever you feel like snacking, as well as just before you sit down for a meal. They'll fill you up and keep you from overeating when you get really hungry.

BLACK MAGIC

CALORIES: 96	CARBS: 22 grams
PROTEINS: 4 grams	FATS: 1.5 grams

½ cup blackberries

½ cup raspberries

1 cup coarsely chopped redbor kale

1 cup cold water

HERBALICIOUS SPINACH

CALORIES: 180	CARBS: 45 grams
PROTEINS: 2.5 grams	FATS: 0 grams

½ cup spinach

½ cup coarsely chopped kale

1 medium apple

½ cup chopped carrots

½ small cucumber, peeled

½ celery stalk

½ small/medium orange

10 parsley sprigs

8 mint leaves

1 cup cold water (or less depending on the juiciness of your fruits)

WATERMELON RUSH

CALORIES: 170	CARBS: 42 grams
PROTEINS: 5 grams	FATS: 0 grams

2 cups chopped watermelon

1 small/medium orange, peeled

1 cup coarsely chopped kale

½ cup water

ice, to taste

LOW-FAT STRAWBERRY BANANA BLAST

CALORIES: 193	CARBS: 27 grams
PROTEINS: 10 grams	FATS: 4 grams

½ banana

½ cup hulled strawberries

½ cup coarsely chopped kale

½ cup whole-milk Greek yogurt

water

ice, to taste

CANTALOUPE LIFTER

CALORIES: 176	CARBS: 45 grams
PROTEINS: 3 grams	FATS: 0 grams

1 cup chopped cantaloupe

1 banana

10 parsley sprigs

1 cup coarsely chopped Swiss chard

1 cup water

ice, to taste

MANGO-MINT ENERGY BOOSTER

CALORIES: 200	CARBS: 33 grams
PROTEINS: 8 grams	FATS: 5 grams

1 cup chopped mango

½ cup whole-milk Greek yogurt

8 mint leaves

water, to taste

BERRY BLASTER

CALORIES: 200	CARBS: 30 grams
PROTEINS: 10 grams	FATS: 6 grams

½ cup raspberries

½ cup blackberries

½ cup blueberries

½ cup whole-milk Greek yogurt

½ cup coarsely chopped Swiss chard

1 cup cold water

ice, to taste

GUAVA GOODNESS

CALORIES: 161	CARBS: 35 grams
PROTEINS: 6 grams	FATS: 1 gram

½ cup chopped guava

½ banana

1 cup spinach

½ cup nonfat soy milk

water and ice, to taste

BERRY BODY DETOXIFIER

CALORIES: 167	CARBS: 28 grams
PROTEINS: 5 grams	FATS: 5 grams

½ cup hulled strawberries

½ cup raspberries

1 celery stalk

1 small cucumber, peeled

½ cup coarsely chopped kale

2 tablespoons chia seeds

cold water, to taste

PROTEIN POWERHOUSE

CALORIES: 199	CARBS: 31 grams
PROTEINS: 13 grams	FATS: 2 grams

1 cup hulled strawberries

¼ cup whole-milk Greek yogurt

¼ cup cooked lentils, cooled

water, to taste

TANGY STRAWBERRY LIMEADE

CALORIES: 169	CARBS: 48 grams
PROTEINS: 5 grams	FATS: 0 grams

1 cup hulled strawberries

1½ cups lime juice

1 cup arugula

1 cup coconut water

SKINNY AVOCADO

CALORIES: 197	**CARBS:** 28 grams
PROTEINS: 4 grams	**FATS:** 8 grams

½ cup hulled strawberries

½ cup blueberries

1 ounce açaí puree or powder

¼ avocado, peeled and pitted

1 cup spinach

½ cup coconut water

cold water, to taste

KAILUA SUNRISE

CALORIES: 178	**CARBS:** 44 grams
PROTEINS: 5 grams	**FATS:** 0 grams

1 small papaya

½ cup chopped pineapple

½ banana

1 cup spinach

½ cup coconut water

cold water, to taste

CHOCOLATY DELIGHT

CALORIES: 184	**CARBS:** 30 grams
PROTEINS: 10 grams	**FATS:** 4 grams

½ cup blueberries

¼ ounce dark chocolate

¼ cup cooked lentils, cooled

water, to taste

ALMOND CRUSH

CALORIES: 190	**CARBS:** 29 grams
PROTEINS: 6 grams	**FATS:** 7 grams

1 cup hulled strawberries

½ banana

¼ cup blanched raw almonds

1 cup coarsely chopped Swiss chard or spinach

cold water, to taste

SWEET BLACK BEAN

CALORIES: 178	**CARBS:** 38 grams
PROTEINS: 8 grams	**FATS:** 2 grams

1 cup blackberries

½ banana

1 cup spinach

¼ cup cooked black beans, cooled

water, to taste

CAN'T BE BEET

CALORIES: 184	**CARBS:** 48 grams
PROTEINS: 8 grams	**FATS:** 0 grams

1 medium pear

1 teaspoon peeled, minced fresh ginger

1 cup coarsely chopped kale

1 cup peeled, chopped raw beets

1 cup lime juice

water, to taste

AUTUMN SUNSET

CALORIES: 198	CARBS: 47 grams
PROTEINS: 6 grams	FATS: 0 grams

3 apricots, pitted

1 medium peach, pitted and chopped

½ banana

1 cup coarsely chopped kale

water, to taste

KIWI COOLER

CALORIES: 194	CARBS: 30 grams
PROTEINS: 5 grams	FATS: 8 grams

1 medium kiwi, peeled

½ banana

1 celery stalk

2 tablespoons ground flaxseed

½ cup almond milk

water, to taste

FAST AND HEALTHY BREAKFAST

CALORIES: 177	CARBS: 27 grams
PROTEINS: 8 grams	FATS: 2 grams

1 cup hulled strawberries

1 tablespoon honey

½ cup whole-milk Greek yogurt

water, to taste

TWELVE
CARB-LOADING SMOOTHIES

The smoothies in this section are loaded with healthy complex carbohydrates, making them the ideal drinks to help you prepare for tomorrow's strenuous workout, game or race. If you're facing a particularly tough physical test, like a 10k, century bike ride or marathon, you should keep in mind that you should be loading up on carbs for a couple days before. Your muscles store carbohydrates as glycogen in the muscles, and your muscles can only absorb so much glycogen at one time, so you should distribute your carb intake over several meals and over several days.

The smoothies in this section are aimed at providing you with at least 50 grams of healthy complex carbs. Your best smoothie-based sources are starches like sweet potatoes, oats, quinoa, beans and lentils, and hearty fruits like bananas and plantains.

SWEET POTATO PIE

CALORIES: 405	CARBS: 71 grams
PROTEINS: 15 grams	FATS: 8 grams

½ cup mashed or sliced sweet potato*

1 banana

2 cups soy milk

dash of ground cinnamon

natural sweetener, to taste

* *Bake sweet potato in oven for about 1 hour at 350°F. Allow to cool in refrigerator overnight.*

GREEN GREEK

CALORIES: 491	CARBS: 61 grams
PROTEINS: 24 grams	FATS: 19.5 grams

1 banana

1 cup spinach

1 cup whole-milk Greek yogurt

¼ cup rolled oats, raw or cooked

2 tablespoons chia seeds

1 cup almond milk

water, to taste

PEANUT BUTTER-BANANA CHOCOLATE DREAM

CALORIES: 740	**CARBS:** 58 grams
PROTEINS: 25 grams	**FATS:** 48.5 grams

1 banana

1 handful spinach (optional)

¼ cup natural peanut butter

1 ounce dark chocolate or 2 tablespoons cacao powder

¼ cup whole-milk Greek yogurt

1 cup almond milk

water, to taste

ALMONDO

CALORIES: 531	**CARBS:** 57 grams
PROTEINS: 14 grams	**FATS:** 29.5 grams

1 banana

1 cup spinach

¼ cup rolled oats, raw or cooked

⅛ cup blanched raw almonds

2 tablespoons natural almond butter

dash of ground cinnamon

1 cup almond milk

water and ice, to taste

BETTER THAN PUMPKIN PIE SMOOTHIE

CALORIES: 289	**CARBS:** 54 grams
PROTEINS: 8 grams	**FATS:** 5 grams

1 cup pumpkin*

1 cup sweet potato*

2 cups almond milk

ground cinnamon, to taste

* Bake pumpkin and sweet potato in 350°F oven for about 1 hour. Allow to cool in refrigerator overnight.

BANANA-BLUEBERRY BLAST

CALORIES: 432	**CARBS:** 87 grams
PROTEINS: 16 grams	**FATS:** 6.5 grams

1 banana

1 cup blueberries

½ cup dandelion greens

1 cup arugula

½ cup whole-milk Greek yogurt

½ cup bran flakes

1 cup coconut water

water, to taste

BEAN THERE DONE THAT

CALORIES: 585	CARBS: 48.5 grams
PROTEINS: 22.5 grams	FATS: 36 grams

½ avocado, peeled and pitted

½ cup spinach

¼ cup cooked black beans, cooled

1 ounce dark chocolate

½ cup whole-milk Greek yogurt

honey, to taste

1 cup soy milk

water and ice, to taste

GO NUTS!

CALORIES: 519	CARBS: 55 grams
PROTEINS: 17 grams	FATS: 29 grams

1 banana

¼ cup rolled oats, raw or cooked

⅛ cup raw walnuts

⅛ cup raw pecans

½ cup whole-milk Greek yogurt

1 cup almond milk

water, ice and salt, to taste

SWEET POTATO-ORANGE SMOOTHIE

CALORIES: 300	CARBS: 63 grams
PROTEINS: 7 grams	FATS: 2.5 grams

1 cup mashed sweet potato*

2 medium oranges, peeled

ground cinnamon, to taste

1 cup almond milk

water, to taste

Bake sweet potato in oven for about 1 hour at 350°F. Allow to cool in refrigerator overnight.

THANKSGIVING PIE SMOOTHIE

CALORIES: 345	CARBS: 54.5 grams
PROTEINS: 7.5 grams	FATS: 12.5 grams

½ cup mashed sweet potato*

1 banana

½ cup coarsely chopped kale

½ cup spinach

⅛ cup raw pecans

1 cup almond milk

Bake sweet potato in oven for about 1 hour at 350°F. Allow to cool in refrigerator overnight.

CARIBBEAN APPLE

CALORIES: 348	CARBS: 84 grams
PROTEINS: 3 grams	FATS: 2.5 grams

½ cup mashed plantain, baked or raw

1 banana

1 apple

dash of ground cinnamon

¼ teaspoon peeled, minced fresh ginger

1 cup almond milk

WHITE BEANS & PEACH BLAST

CALORIES: 386	CARBS: 63 grams
PROTEINS: 13 grams	FATS: 10 grams

1 cup peaches

½ cup cooked white beans, cooled

⅛ cup blanched raw almonds

dash of ground cinnamon

dash of ground nutmeg

1 cup rice milk

water and ice, to taste

CREAMY MANGO & PAPAYA SMOOTHIE

CALORIES: 496	**CARBS:** 73 grams
PROTEINS: 26 grams	**FATS:** 14 grams

1 small papaya, peeled and seeded

1 cup chopped mango

½ cup cooked white beans, cooled

1 cup whole-milk Greek yogurt

1 cup almond milk

water and ice, to taste

RICH CHOCOLATE BEAN COOLER

CALORIES: 527	**CARBS:** 53 grams
PROTEINS: 14 grams	**FATS:** 31 grams

½ avocado, peeled and pitted

1 cup spinach

¼ cup cooked black beans, cooled

¼ cup rolled oats, raw or cooked

1 ounce dark chocolate

1 tablespoon honey

1 cup almond milk

water and ice, to taste

SWEET POTATO PA-PIE-A

CALORIES: 393.5	**CARBS:** 63.5 grams
PROTEINS: 17.5 grams	**FATS:** 9.5 grams

1 cup mashed sweet potato*

1 small papaya, peeled and seeded

½ banana

½ cup whole-milk Greek yogurt

1 cup soy milk

Bake sweet potato in oven for about 1 hour at 350°F. Allow to cool in refrigerator overnight.

THIRTEEN
ENERGY-BOOSTING SMOOTHIES

Getting ready to start a long workout—whether it's a mile-long swim, a 50-mile bike ride or an Ironman—requires an abundance of mental and physical energy and smoothies packed with B12 and complex carbohydrates can deliver just the boost you need. If you're under-nourished or under-hydrated, chances are you'll crash before you even get started. The following smoothies are a great way to load up on liquids and fill up on fuels to ensure optimum energy throughout your workout. And remember Grandma's golden rule: Wait 30 minutes after drinking your smoothie before hopping in that pool (or on that bike, trail, field or court). You can use that time to stretch or drive to your workout launch point.

Most fruits and vegetables contain at least some carbohydrates, but you may want to supercharge your smoothie with some grains like rice or rolled oats, or even legumes like black beans or garbanzo beans. You'll also want to pack your smoothies with vitamin B12, which is pretty much only found in fish, meat and dairy products like milk and yogurt. Oh, and one more thing: If you're looking for carb-heavy smoothies, you may want to swap out your Greek yogurt for old-fashioned "regular" yogurt, as "regular" yogurt contains about twice as many carbs as Greek yogurt (around 16 grams of carbs compared to around 8).

ORANGE-BANANA BOOSTER

CALORIES: 523	CARBS: 91 grams
PROTEINS: 43 grams	FATS: 2 grams

2 oranges, peeled
1 banana
¼ cup plain whole-milk yogurt
½ cup bran flakes
¼ cup egg white powder
1 cup milk
ice, to taste

ON THE MANGO

CALORIES: 438	CARBS: 73 grams
PROTEINS: 33 grams	FATS: 3 grams

1 cup chopped mango
½ banana
½ cup spinach
½ cup alfalfa sprouts
¼ cup rolled oats, raw or cooked
1 scoop casein protein powder
1 cup coconut water
water and ice, to taste

BERRY BURST

CALORIES: 445	CARBS: 93 grams
PROTEINS: 22 grams	FATS: 2.5 grams

½ cup blackberries

½ cup hulled strawberries

½ cup raspberries

½ cup blueberries

½ banana

½ cup bran flakes

1 cup plain whole-milk yogurt

1 cup coconut water

SWEET POTATO-SPINACH SUNRISE

CALORIES: 546	CARBS: 88 grams
PROTEINS: 25 grams	FATS: 11.5 grams

1 cup spinach

1 banana

½ cup mashed sweet potato*

½ cup rolled oats, raw or cooked

1 cup plain whole-milk yogurt

1 cup almond milk

¼ cup blanched raw almonds

* *Bake sweet potato in oven for about 1 hour at 350°F. Allow to cool in refrigerator overnight.*

KIWI KRUSH

CALORIES: 445	CARBS: 71 grams
PROTEINS: 12.5 grams	FATS: 14 grams

3 medium kiwis, peeled
½ cup blueberries
½ avocado, pitted and peeled
½ cup dandelion greens
½ cup plain whole-milk yogurt
1 medium orange, peeled
1 cup water
ice, to taste

Optional addition: This smoothie works well with plain and vanilla protein powders.

BERRY BEAN BLAST

CALORIES: 585	CARBS: 104 grams
PROTEINS: 43 grams	FATS: 1 gram

1 cup blackberries
1 cup chopped mango
1 banana
¼ cup cooked lentils, cooled
½ cup plain whole-milk yogurt
¼ cup egg white powder
1 cup coconut water

ICY RICE RUSH

CALORIES: 501	CARBS: 95 grams
PROTEINS: 14 grams	FATS: 9 grams

½ banana

½ cup hulled strawberries

1 medium orange, peeled

½ cup whole-milk Greek yogurt

½ cup cooked white or brown rice, cooled

1 tablespoon honey (optional)

1 cup rice milk

ice, to taste

CHERRY, PINEAPPLE AND WHITE BEAN SMOOTHIE

CALORIES: 439	CARBS: 73 grams
PROTEINS: 16 grams	FATS: 12.5 grams

½ cup tart cherries, pitted

1 cup chopped pineapple

½ banana

½ cup cooked white beans, cooled

2 tablespoons ground flaxseed

water and ice, to taste

Optional addition: This smoothie works well with protein powders.

FOURTEEN

PROTEIN-ENRICHED POST-WORKOUT SMOOTHIES

Ready to pack on muscle or make sure you're maintaining what you've got? The following 25 smoothies have been crafted to maximize protein intake so that you end up with approximately 30 grams of protein in each smoothie, roughly the maximum amount that your body can process after a single meal. In addition to protein, these smoothies offer a balance of good carbs and fat intake so you have the proper caloric balance to add lean, healthy muscle mass.

In order to hit 30 grams of protein per serving, each of these smoothies uses some sort of protein-rich supplement (from whey and casein to egg whites and Greek yogurt) in addition to plant-protein-rich ingredients (see the "Protein and Other Smoothie Supplements" chapter, page 88, for a nutritional breakdown of each protein addition). While you can add protein powders or boosters to any of the other smoothie recipes in this book, these 25 recipes have been tweaked to work (taste- and texture-wise) with each listed supplement. Finally, remember, if you are trying to build muscle and are shooting to consume over 100 grams of protein per day, you should try to limit your protein supplement intake to just one serving per day. Keep in mind that doubling up on protein supplements can have adverse effects on the body.

DAIRY-BASED SMOOTHIES

RASPBERRY CREAM

CALORIES: 330	CARBS: 19 grams
PROTEINS: 27 grams	FATS: 17.5 grams

½ cup raspberries

½ avocado, peeled and pitted

¼ cup egg white powder

1 cup almond milk

POMEGRANATE PUNCH

CALORIES: 577	CARBS: 83 grams
PROTEINS: 22 grams	FATS: 21.5 grams

½ cup raspberries

½ cup blackberries

½ cup hulled strawberries

½ cup blueberries

1 cup Greek whole-milk yogurt

¼ cup chia seeds

1 cup pomegranate juice

ANGEL'S EGGNOG

CALORIES: 486	CARBS: 68 grams
PROTEINS: 30 grams	FATS: 10.5 grams

2 bananas

½ pinch ground cinnamon

½ pinch ground nutmeg

¼ cup chia seeds

¼ cup egg white powder

1 cup almond milk

MANGO MUSCLE

CALORIES: 502	**CARBS:** 68 grams
PROTEINS: 23 grams	**FATS:** 20 grams

1 cup chopped mango

½ cup chopped pineapple

¼ cup chia seeds

¼ cup lime juice

1 cup chopped silken tofu

1 cup whole-milk Greek yogurt

1 cup water

STAR FRUIT SMOOTHIE

CALORIES: 470	**CARBS:** 57 grams
PROTEINS: 26 grams	**FATS:** 19 grams

2 small star fruits (carambola), peeled and chopped

1 banana

1 cup Greek whole-milk yogurt

1 cup whole dairy milk

PEACHES 'N' CREAM

CALORIES: 492	**CARBS:** 76 grams
PROTEINS: 25 grams	**FATS:** 12 grams

2 medium peaches, pitted and chopped

1 banana

2 tablespoons chia seeds

2 tablespoons egg white powder

1 cup whole dairy milk

PLUM BOX

CALORIES: 349	CARBS: 45 grams
PROTEINS: 29 grams	FATS: 6 grams

2 medium plums, pitted

½ cup chopped mango

1 cup spinach

2 tablespoons ground flaxseed

¼ cup egg white powder

1 cup coconut water

COCONUT-PINEAPPLE PASSION

CALORIES: 414	CARBS: 60 grams
PROTEINS: 30 grams	FATS: 8 grams

1 cup chopped pineapple

½ cup passion fruit pulp

¼ cup coconut meat

¼ cup egg white powder

1 cup coconut water

APRICOT CUCUMBER COOLER

CALORIES: 584	CARBS: 72 grams
PROTEINS: 25 grams	FATS: 25.5 grams

3 small or medium apricots, pitted

1 small cucumber, unpeeled

1 cup chopped mango

½ banana

¼ cup chia seeds

1 cup whole-milk Greek yogurt

1 cup almond milk

CUCUMBER AND BERRY BLEND

CALORIES: 321	CARBS: 48 grams
PROTEINS: 31 grams	FATS: 1.5 grams

½ cup blackberries

½ cup raspberries

1 small cucumber, peeled

½ banana

1 cup coarsely chopped kale

¼ cup egg white powder

1 cup coconut water

KIWI-CUCUMBER REFRESHER

CALORIES: 289	CARBS: 30 grams
PROTEINS: 27 grams	FATS: 7 grams

1 medium kiwi, peeled

1 small cucumber

½ banana

1 cup spinach

¼ cup egg white powder

2 tablespoons coconut milk

water, to taste

PIÑA CU-LADA

CALORIES: 416	CARBS: 62 grams
PROTEINS: 29 grams	FATS: 7 grams

1 cup chopped pineapple

1 small cucumber, peeled

1 banana

¼ cup egg white powder

2 tablespoons coconut milk

1 cup coconut water

BLUES BLASTER

CALORIES: 318	**CARBS:** 42 grams
PROTEINS: 29 grams	**FATS:** 3 grams

1 cup blueberries

¼ cup whole-milk Greek yogurt

1 tablespoon honey

1 scoop whey protein

water, to taste

SUMMER SALAD

CALORIES: 302	**CARBS:** 42 grams
PROTEINS: 27 grams	**FATS:** 3.5 grams

1 cup hulled strawberries

1 medium apple, pared

1 cup spinach

1 scoop whey protein

1 cup almond milk

VEGETARIAN AND VEGAN SUPPLEMENT SMOOTHIES

Vegan and vegetarian protein powder supplements tend to be a bit grittier and more unpleasant than dairy-based supplements. And your reaction to these smoothies could range from mild dislike to considering your concoction downright undrinkable. But if you're an athlete on a plant-based diet, these supplements can be a necessary evil. To combat the grittiness, we highly recommend blending in ingredients that will make your smoothie richer and creamier to help absorb any unpleasant taste or texture. Some prime candidates are bananas, plantains, avocados and mangoes.

In addition to taste, keep in mind that plant-based supplements tend not to provide the same amount of complete protein as dairy-based supplements, normally giving you about 15 grams compared to about 24 grams for a dairy alternative. In order to max out your protein intake after a tough workout at around 30 grams, you should plan on including protein-rich plants like legumes, nuts and greens in your recipes.

THE RED RED RED SMOOTHIE

CALORIES: 364	CARBS: 67 grams
PROTEINS: 20 grams	FATS: 3 grams

1 cup chopped watermelon
1 cup hulled strawberries
½ grapefruit, peeled
½ banana
1 teaspoon peeled, minced fresh ginger
1 scoop mixed-plant protein (Vega One)
½ cup coconut water

BLACKBERRY BONANZA

CALORIES: 474	CARBS: 61 grams
PROTEINS: 29 grams	FATS: 15 grams

1 cup blackberries

½ banana

¼ cup blanched raw almonds

1 cup coarsely chopped kale

1 scoop mixed-plant protein (Vega One)

1 cup soy milk

CARIBBEAN BLISS

CALORIES: 493	CARBS: 78 grams
PROTEINS: 22 grams	FATS: 11 grams

½ cup sliced cooked plantains, cooled

½ cup chopped mango

¼ cup chia seeds

1 scoop mixed-plant protein (Vega One)

1 cup coconut water

CANTALOUPE FLUSH

CALORIES: 408	CARBS: 62 grams
PROTEINS: 22 grams	FATS: 9.5 grams

1 cup chopped cantaloupe

1 cup hulled strawberries

½ banana

1 cup beet greens

2 tablespoons chia seeds

1 scoop mixed-plant protein (Vega One)

1 cup almond milk

PEACH AND AVOCADO BREEZE

CALORIES: 516	CARBS: 75 grams
PROTEINS: 21 grams	FATS: 17 grams

1 medium peach, pitted and chopped

1 banana

½ avocado, peeled and pitted

1 small orange, peeled

1 cup spinach

1 scoop mixed-plant protein (Vega One)

water, to taste

CHOCOLATE MONSTER MILKSHAKE
(HIGH-CALORIE SOY OPTION)

CALORIES: 697	CARBS: 65 grams
PROTEINS: 35 grams	FATS: 38 grams

1 banana

½ avocado, peeled and pitted

1 ounce dark chocolate

1 scoop soy protein

2 tablespoons coconut milk

1 cup soy milk

EASY BREEZY
(LOW-CALORIE SOY OPTION)

CALORIES: 242	CARBS: 35 grams
PROTEINS: 28 grams	FATS: 1 gram

1 cup hulled strawberries

1 small orange, peeled

1 cup spinach

1 scoop soy protein

1 cup coconut water

NECTAR OF THE GODS

CALORIES: 391	**CARBS:** 76 grams
PROTEINS: 29 grams	**FATS:** 2 grams

1 medium nectarine, pitted

½ cup raspberries

1 banana

1 cup coarsely chopped kale

1 tablespoon honey

1 scoop soy protein

water, to taste

CHOCOLATE, STRAWBERRIES & SPICE

CALORIES: 390	**CARBS:** 40 grams
PROTEINS: 24.5 grams	**FATS:** 14.5 grams

½ cup hulled strawberries

1 cup arugula

¼ cup cooked lentils, cooled

1 ounce dark chocolate

1 scoop rice protein

1 cup almond milk

SWEET BEANS 'N' RICE

CALORIES: 340	CARBS: 56 grams
PROTEINS: 23 grams	FATS: 3.5 grams

1 cup blueberries

½ banana

1 cup spinach

½ cup cooked black beans, cooled

1 tablespoon honey

1 scoop rice protein

water, to taste

SEPTEMBER SUN

CALORIES: 380	CARBS: 74 grams
PROTEINS: 30 grams	FATS: 5 grams

½ cup chopped pineapple

½ cup passion fruit pulp

¼ cup cooked white beans, cooled

1 scoop rice protein

1 cup soy milk

15 OVER 500: CALORIE-DENSE SMOOTHIES

If you're looking to gain muscle mass (or just gain extra weight), you need to eat a lot of calories every single day. Smoothies make an excellent way to ingest big calorie blocks efficiently and easily, especially if you're short on time (or appetite). The following 15 smoothies all pack over 500 calories that ensure you take in an even balance of all macronutrients. Remember that your body relies on more than protein to build muscle and gain weight. You also need ample amounts of carbohydrates and healthy fats to ensure your body has the energy it needs and won't consume valuable muscle mass to make up for any deficiencies.

The following smoothies are especially good for morning meals or just after a workout. If you plan on adding a protein supplement to any of the smoothies in this section, keep in mind that your body will only process a maximum of about 30 grams of protein at a time, so adjust your supplement additions to blend with the protein count already provided by the smoothie's natural ingredients.

A WORD OF WISDOM: BEANS AND EXERCISE DON'T MIX!

By now you probably know that during periods of intense exercise, your body is going to rely primarily on carbohydrates and fats to power through and that you should save most of your proteins for after the workout. This strategy is especially true when it comes to adding beans to your smoothies—you should always wait until after your workouts (or at least six hours *before* your workout) to enjoy a smoothie that includes any legumes. Beans are particularly heavy on protein and dietary fiber, a combination that can make you feel sluggish and uncomfortable, especially if your workout includes intense cardio.

PB&G SMOOTHIE

CALORIES: 601	CARBS: 55 grams
PROTEINS: 24 grams	FATS: 36 grams

1 banana
1 cup spinach
10 sprigs parsley
¼ cup crunchy natural peanut butter
1 cup soy milk
ice cubes or water, to taste

CHOCOLATE-ALMOND BURST

CALORIES: 513	CARBS: 49 grams
PROTEINS: 13 grams	FATS: 30 grams

1 banana

1 cup spinach

1 tablespoon natural almond butter

1 ounce dark chocolate

⅛ cup blanched raw almonds

¼ cup whole-milk Greek yogurt

dash of ground cinnamon

½ cup cold water

ice, to taste

AUTUMN'S CORNUCOPIA

CALORIES: 602	CARBS: 76 grams
PROTEINS: 13 grams	FATS: 29 grams

½ cup sweet potato*

½ cup raspberries

½ cup hulled strawberries

1 banana

¼ cup chia seeds

¼ cup raw walnuts

1 cup almond milk

Bake sweet potato in oven for about 1 hour at 350°F. Allow to cool in refrigerator overnight.

KINGSTON BLEND

CALORIES: 547	**CARBS:** 105 grams
PROTEINS: 9 grams	**FATS:** 16 grams

1 cup chopped mango

1 cup cooked sliced plantains, cooled

1 cup spinach

¼ cup chia seeds

2 tablespoons coconut milk

water, to taste

DREAMY AND CREAMY

CALORIES: 550	**CARBS:** 70 grams
PROTEINS: 19 grams	**FATS:** 24 grams

1 cup chopped mango

1 banana

½ avocado, peeled and pitted

1 cup spinach

1 cup whole-milk Greek yogurt

water, to taste

MIXING BOWL

CALORIES: 510	CARBS: 104 grams
PROTEINS: 12 grams	FATS: 9 grams

1 cup chopped apple

1 cup chopped pineapple

1 medium kiwi, peeled

1 banana

1 cup coarsely chopped kale

1 cup spinach

¼ cup chia seeds

1 cup coconut water

APRICOTS AND PROTEIN

CALORIES: 555	CARBS: 112 grams
PROTEINS: 27 grams	FATS: 14 grams

1 cup pitted and chopped apricots

1 banana

1 cup arugula

½ cup cooked white beans, cooled

¼ cup rolled oats, raw or cooked

2 tablespoons coconut milk

1 cup almond milk

SAVORY STRAWBERRY

CALORIES: 505	**CARBS:** 71 grams
PROTEINS: 21 grams	**FATS:** 18 grams

1 cup hulled strawberries

1 banana

1 cup spinach

½ cup cooked black beans, cooled

¼ cup flaxseed

¼ cup whole-milk Greek yogurt

1 cup almond milk

EARTHY, SEEDY AND SAVORY

CALORIES: 536	**CARBS:** 60 grams
PROTEINS: 20 grams	**FATS:** 30 grams

1 cup hulled strawberries

¼ cup flaxseed

½ avocado, peeled and pitted

1 cup beet greens

¼ cup cooked lentils, cooled

2 cups water, or to taste

COCONUT-OAT-MAC SMOOTHIE

CALORIES: 521	**CARBS:** 79 grams
PROTEINS: 10 grams	**FATS:** 30 grams

1 banana

¼ cup rolled oats, raw or cooked

¼ cup macadamia nuts

2 tablespoons coconut milk

1 cup coconut water

RED BEAN REVIVER

CALORIES: 538	**CARBS:** 83 grams
PROTEINS: 26 grams	**FATS:** 14 grams

½ cup hulled strawberries

½ cup raspberries

1 banana

1 cup coarsely chopped kale

¼ cup cooked red beans, cooled

¼ cup ground hemp seeds

1 cup coconut water

SUMMER RUSH

CALORIES: 528	CARBS: 81 grams
PROTEINS: 19 grams	FATS: 18 grams

½ cup raspberries

½ cup blackberries

½ cup blueberries

½ cup hulled strawberries

1 banana

¼ cup cooked lentils, cooled

¼ cup blanched raw almonds

1 cup almond milk

water and ice, to taste

TROPICAL CARB LOADER

CALORIES: 560	CARBS: 114 grams
PROTEINS: 11 grams	FATS: 13 grams

1 small papaya

1 cup chopped pineapple

1 cup cooked sliced plantains, cooled

1 cup spinach

⅛ cup raw cashews

2 tablespoons coconut milk

1 cup coconut water

AMOUR D'ÉTÉ

CALORIES: 504	CARBS: 101 grams
PROTEINS: 11 grams	FATS: 26 grams

1 peach, pitted and chopped

1 banana

½ cup raspberries

3 hulled strawberries

2 tablespoons raw pine nuts

2 tablespoons chia seeds

1 cup almond milk

GREEN CHARGER

CALORIES: 521	CARBS: 117 grams
PROTEINS: 12 grams	FATS: 28 grams

1 medium kiwi, peeled

1 medium apple

½ avocado, pitted and peeled

1 cup spinach

¼ cup cooked lentils, cooled

2 tablespoons chia seeds

2 tablespoons coconut milk

1 cup almond milk

SIXTEEN

EVENING SMOOTHIES

Whether you are looking to unwind after a long day or need help falling asleep after an energizing late-night workout, a delicious, soothing smoothie is the perfect pre-bedtime snack. In addition to keeping you sated throughout the night, a small protein smoothie actually has a fat-busting effect on the body— it will keep your metabolism from slowing down too much overnight.

Packed with special sleep-inducing ingredients such as chamomile (a calming ingredient), magnesium (a sedative) and tryptophan (an amino acid that aids in sleep), these six lightweight smoothies are specially designed to help you fall asleep and rest deeply throughout the night. Cherries, herbal teas, milk and soy milk, pineapples, bananas, oranges, spirulina, spinach and egg whites are some of the best ingredients for nighttime smoothies. Because you don't want to consume too much fat just before bed, the recipes in this section call for nonfat or low-fat dairy options instead of the typical whole-fat options normally used.

CHERRY SLUMBER

CALORIES: 371	CARBS: 77 grams
PROTEINS: 13 grams	FATS: 13.5 grams

1 cup tart cherries, pitted
1 banana
1 tablespoon spirulina powder
1 tablespoon honey
1 cup soy milk
water and ice, to taste

CHAMOMILE CRUSH

CALORIES: 378	CARBS: 57 grams
PROTEINS: 16 grams	FATS: 11 grams

1 banana
⅛ cup blanched raw almonds
¼ cup nonfat Greek yogurt
ground cinnamon, to taste
1 tablespoon maple syrup
1 cup soy milk
1 cup prepared chamomile tea, chilled
ice, to taste

MILKY WAY

CALORIES: 346	**CARBS:** 56 grams
PROTEINS: 14 grams	**FATS:** 10 grams

½ cup tart cherries, pitted

½ banana

⅛ cup chopped raw walnuts

1 tablespoon honey

1 cup warm low-fat milk

dash of ground nutmeg

ORANGE-PINEAPPLE CHAMOMILE TEA

CALORIES: 136	**CARBS:** 27 grams
PROTEINS: 5 grams	**FATS:** 2 grams

1 orange, peeled

½ cup chopped pineapple

½ inch peeled, fresh ginger

dash of ground cinnamon

1 cup prepared chamomile tea, chilled

½ cup soy milk

ice, to taste

SPINACH AND SPIRULINA SLEEPY TIME

CALORIES: 193	CARBS: 45 grams
PROTEINS: 7 grams	FATS: 1 gram

1 peach, pitted and chopped

1 banana

1 cup spinach

1 tablespoon spirulina powder

1 tablespoon honey (optional)

1 cup prepared chamomile tea, chilled

ice, to taste

COCONUT SPINACH SPIKE

CALORIES: 163	CARBS: 33.5 grams
PROTEINS: 9 grams	FATS: 0 grams

½ cup spinach

juice of 1 lemon

¼ cup nonfat Greek yogurt

1 tablespoon honey

pinch of sea salt

1 cup coconut water

CASEIN-HEAVY BEDTIME SMOOTHIES

If you're serious about gaining muscle mass, a late-night casein-based protein smoothie is essential—the slow-absorbing casein will deliver your body time-released protein throughout the entire night. Since gaining muscle mass and strength is all about allowing the body to repair itself, and since most of your body's repairing goes on after you fall asleep, charging yourself with those essential amino acids just before dozing off can have a dramatic effect on your strength training.

The key, however, to a good bedtime smoothie is simplicity. You don't want to raise your blood sugar levels, which will make it more difficult to sleep.

STRAWBERRIES 'N' CREAM

CALORIES: 169	CARBS: 15 grams
PROTEINS: 25 grams	FATS: 1 gram

1 cup hulled strawberries
½ teaspoon vanilla extract
1 scoop vanilla casein protein
1 cup cool water

GREEN DREAM

CALORIES: 400	CARBS: 59 grams
PROTEINS: 34 grams	FATS: 5 grams

1 banana
1 cup coarsely chopped kale
1 cup chopped pineapple
1 scoop casein powder
1 cup soy milk

KING KONG

CALORIES: 307	CARBS: 55 grams
PROTEINS: 21 grams	FATS: 2 grams

1 banana
2 cups low-fat milk

SLEEPER CAR

CALORIES: 387	CARBS: 53 grams
PROTEINS: 30 grams	FATS: 8 grams

1 banana
1 medium orange, peeled
1 cup spinach
1 scoop casein powder
2 tablespoons coconut milk
1 cup coconut water

SUN BELT

CALORIES: 272	CARBS: 41 grams
PROTEINS: 28 grams	FATS: 1 gram

1 cup chopped pineapple
1 medium orange, peeled
1 cup coarsely chopped kale
1 scoop casein powder
water, to taste

SEVENTEEN

ANTI-INFLAMMATORY SMOOTHIES

These smoothies are ideal for right after a long, brutal workout or tough game when your body is hurting. Each of the ingredients in the smoothies has powerful anti-inflammatory properties that will help soothe your muscles and joints and prevent swelling. If you're making your own concoction, the best ingredients for anti-inflammatory smoothies are foods rich in omega-3 fatty acids, such as flaxseeds and walnuts, certain spices like ginger, turmeric, cinnamon and teas, and some colorful fruits and vegetables such as spicy peppers, beets, tart cherries, blueberries and dark leafy greens.

Important note: Some people experience a sensitivity to the solanine found in blueberries, artichokes and nightshade plants (tomatoes, potatoes, eggplants and peppers). People suffering from arthritis and/or joint pain may want to avoid these foods entirely; however, solanine sensitivity is rare, and for most people the antioxidants these fruits and veggies contain more than outweighs the negligible effects of solanine, making them anti-inflammatory.

INFLAMMATION ERASER

CALORIES: 120	CARBS: 29 grams
PROTEINS: 4 grams	FATS: 1 gram

½ cup chopped cantaloupe
½ cup hulled strawberries
½ cup raspberries
1 cup coarsely chopped kale
water to, taste

* *This is an excellent smoothie to add post-workout protein powder to.*

CHEERY CHERRY

CALORIES: 447	CARBS: 40 grams
PROTEINS: 14 grams	FATS: 28 grams

½ cup blueberries
½ cup tart cherries, pitted
2 teaspoons peeled, minced fresh ginger
2 tablespoons flaxseed
¼ cup chopped raw walnuts
1 cup soy milk
water, to taste

LEAFY GREENS & GREEN TEA

CALORIES: 124	**CARBS:** 28 grams
PROTEINS: 4.5 grams	**FATS:** 0 grams

1 cup kale

1 cup spinach

2 inches peeled fresh ginger

½ cup tart cherries, pitted

½ cup blueberries

1 cup green tea, unsweetened

A SPLICE OF SPICE

CALORIES: 127	**CARBS:** 32 grams
PROTEINS: 1 gram	**FATS:** 0 grams

1 small papaya, peeled and pitted

2 teaspoons peeled, minced fresh ginger

½ teaspoon ground turmeric

½ teaspoon ground cinnamon

dash of cayenne pepper

1 cup prepared black tea, chilled or room temperature

1 tablespoon honey (optional)

ice, as needed

LAVA-CADO SMOOTHIE

CALORIES: 365	CARBS: 34 grams
PROTEINS: 11 grams	FATS: 22.5 grams

½ avocado, pitted and peeled

½ cup blackberries

¼ cup chia seeds

pinch of cayenne pepper

honey, to taste

1 cup soy milk

water and ice, to taste

GREEN, ORANGE & SPICY SMOOTHIE

CALORIES: 413	CARBS: 58 grams
PROTEINS: 9 grams	FATS: 18 grams

2 medium oranges, peeled

½ avocado, pitted and peeled

1 cup spinach

1 cup coarsely chopped kale

½ teaspoon ground turmeric

½ teaspoon ground cinnamon

dash of black pepper

dash of cayenne pepper

2 teaspoons peeled, minced fresh ginger

2 tablespoons chia seeds

1 tablespoon maple syrup

water and ice, to taste

BLUEBERRY-BASIL BEET BLAST

CALORIES: 382	CARBS: 41 grams
PROTEINS: 8.5 grams	FATS: 23 grams

½ cup blueberries

½ avocado, pitted and peeled

½ banana

1 cup beet greens

½ cup boiled, chopped beets

¼ cup basil (about 10 leaves)

dash of ground cinnamon

dash of ground turmeric

1 tablespoon natural almond butter

water and ice, to taste

WALNUT-AVOCADO SMOOTHIE

CALORIES: 522	CARBS: 49 grams
PROTEINS: 11 grams	FATS: 34.5 grams

½ avocado, pitted and peeled

1 cup blueberries

½ banana

1 cup spinach

1 cup arugula

¼ cup raw walnuts

1 cup almond milk

water, to taste

CHERRY-BANANA INFLAMMATION BLASTER

CALORIES: 376	**CARBS:** 69 grams
PROTEINS: 11 grams	**FATS:** 8 grams

½ cup tart cherries, pitted

1 banana

1 cup spinach

2 tablespoons chia seeds

½ teaspoon ground turmeric

dash of cayenne pepper

1 cup soy milk

1 tablespoon maple syrup

water and ice, to taste

THE RED INFLAMMATION REDUCER

CALORIES: 376	**CARBS:** 61 grams
PROTEINS: 9.5 grams	**FATS:** 14 grams

½ cup boiled, chopped beets

½ banana

½ avocado, peeled and pitted

½ cup tart cherries, pitted

1 cup beet greens

½ cup chopped mango

1 cup coconut water

water, to taste

EIGHTEEN

HYDRATING SMOOTHIES

A simple, refreshing smoothie packed with hydrating electrolytes, a few carbs and nutrients can make for the ideal sports drink. And if you're the type of athlete who likes long, arduous workouts, you probably know the incredible importance of a midworkout electrolyte break. The alternative, straining your body beyond its capabilities, and known by terms like "hitting the wall," "crashing" "bonking," is not only devastating to your performance, but it can be physiologically extremely dangerous.

The following recipes have the hydrating properties that you'll want midworkout without the nutritional bulk that will slow you down or make you cramp up. They're ideal for before and during a workout and are designed to keep you light and operating at an optimal level. In addition, none of the recipes has the pulp or thick consistency that other green and protein-fortified smoothies do, so they're perfectly portable to the gym, game or trail!

If you're experimenting on your own, you should try making your smoothies out of some of these electrolyte-packed ingredients: coconut water, oranges, plums, melons, a lemon or lime, and, if you want a couple extra carbs and thickness, bananas. To replenish lost salt content, you should also try using a couple pinches of sea salt.

Pro tip: If you find that some of these simpler smoothies aren't integrating well (i.e., the fruit and liquid base are layered), simply add a thickening agent like a half a banana or ½ cup of Greek yogurt.

COCONUT-ORANGE REFRESHER

CALORIES: 136	CARBS: 31 grams
PROTEINS: 4 grams	FATS: 0 grams

2 medium oranges (or 4 to 6 small oranges/
    tangerines), peeled
1 cup coconut water
pinch of sea salt, or to taste
water and ice (optional)

TROPICAL WATERMELON

CALORIES: 92	CARBS: 21 grams
PROTEINS: 3 grams	FATS: 0 grams

1 cup chopped watermelon

1 cup coconut water

pinch of sea salt, or to taste

water and ice (optional)

REFRESHING MELON

CALORIES: 106	CARBS: 25 grams
PROTEINS: 3 grams	FATS: 0 grams

1 cup chopped cantaloupe

1 cup coconut water

pinch of sea salt, or to taste

water and ice (optional)

MANGO-ORANGE QUENCHER

CALORIES: 144	CARBS: 34 grams
PROTEINS: 3.5 grams	FATS: 0 grams

½ cup chopped mango

1 medium orange, peeled

1 cup coconut water

4 ice cubes

COOLING CUCUMBER

CALORIES: 59	**CARBS:** 14 grams
PROTEINS: 1.5 grams	**FATS:** 0 grams

1 small cucumber, peeled
½ cup chopped honeydew melon
juice of ½ small lemon
water and ice, to taste

STRAWBERRY-COCONUT COOLER

CALORIES: 216	**CARBS:** 40 grams
PROTEINS: 6 grams	**FATS:** 4 grams

1 cup hulled strawberries
½ banana
1 cup coconut water
2 tablespoons chia seeds
water and ice, to taste

PEACH PASSION

CALORIES: 220	**CARBS:** 52 grams
PROTEINS: 6 grams	**FATS:** 0 grams

2 medium peaches (pitted and chopped)
½ banana
½ cup spinach
1 cup coconut water
ice, to taste

SOUTHERN LIMEADE

CALORIES: 83	CARBS: 21 grams
PROTEINS: 3 grams	FATS: 0 grams

1 medium lime, peeled or juiced

1 medium lemon, peeled or juiced

1 cup coconut water

water and ice, to taste

MANGO-ORANGE ELECTROLYTE SMOOTHIE

CALORIES: 150	CARBS: 38 grams
PROTEINS: 2.5 grams	FATS: 0 grams

1 medium orange, peeled

½ cup chopped mango

½ banana

pinch of sea salt, or to taste

water and ice, to taste

GINGER-LEMON THIRST QUENCHER

CALORIES: 102	CARBS: 27 grams
PROTEINS: 1 gram	FATS: 0 grams

2 teaspoons peeled, minced fresh ginger

2 lemons, peeled

1 tablespoon honey

pinch of sea salt, or to taste

water and ice, to taste

FRESCA SUBLIME

CALORIES: 158	CARBS: 38 grams
PROTEINS: 4.5 grams	FATS: 0 grams

1 cup hulled strawberries

1 cup chopped watermelon

1 peeled, seeded fresh lemon

pinch of sea salt, or to taste

1 cup coconut water

water and ice, to taste

RASPBERRY LIMEADE

CALORIES: 130	CARBS: 32 grams
PROTEINS: 4.5 grams	FATS: 0 grams

1 cup raspberries

1 medium lime, peeled or juiced

pinch of sea salt, or to taste

1 cup coconut water

water and ice, to taste

LEMON ELECTROLYTE SMOOTHIE

CALORIES: 128	CARBS: 34 grams
PROTEINS: 1 gram	FATS: 0 grams

1 medium lemon, peeled or juiced

1 medium tangerine, peeled

1 tablespoon honey

pinch of sea salt, or to taste

water and ice, to taste

NO-SLUMBER CUCUMBER

CALORIES: 196	CARBS: 36 grams
PROTEINS: 7.5 grams	FATS: 2 grams

1 small cucumber, peeled

1 medium lemon, peeled or juiced

¼ cup whole-milk Greek yogurt

1 tablespoon honey

pinch of sea salt, or to taste

1 cup coconut water

water and ice, to taste

ORANGE-SWEET POTATO RECHARGER

CALORIES: 187	CARBS: 45 grams
PROTEINS: 4 grams	FATS: 0 grams

¼ cup sweet potato*

½ banana

2 medium oranges, peeled

dash of ground cinnamon

water and ice, to taste

Bake sweet potato in oven for about 1 hour at 350°F. Allow to cool in refrigerator overnight.

CELE-RECHARGE

CALORIES: 141	CARBS: 38 grams
PROTEINS: 1.5 grams	FATS: 0 grams

1 celery stalk
1 medium lime, squeezed or juiced
1 pear
1 tablespoon honey
pinch of sea salt, or to taste
water and ice, to taste

NO-CRASH COCONUT

CALORIES: 223	CARBS: 39 grams
PROTEINS: 6 grams	FATS: 7 grams

1 medium orange, peeled
½ banana
½ cup coarsely chopped kale
pinch of sea salt, or to taste
1 cup coconut water
2 tablespoons coconut milk
water and ice, to taste

NINETEEN

IMMUNE-BOOSTING SMOOTHIES

You can't keep your body in peak physical shape if you can't keep it from getting sick. This is especially true when the harsh winter months hit and many physical activities are confined to germ-infested gyms at the same time that cold and flu seasons are at their peak. While keeping your hands clean (and away from your face) while you work out can stave off infection from the outside, consuming immune-boosting fruits and vegetables can work wonders in building up your body's natural defenses. In order to maximize your immunity, spend the winter months drinking smoothies rich in beta-carotene (cantaloupe, carrot, grapefruit, sweet potato, apricot, spinach, tangerine and tomato), vitamin C (berries, kale, kiwi, mango, orange, papaya, strawberry and sweet potato), vitamin E (carrot, turnip greens, mango, nuts and spinach) and zinc (nuts and beans). The following 15 recipes are our tried-and-tested favorites for the cold winter months.

COLD BUSTER

CALORIES: 246	CARBS: 53 grams
PROTEINS: 6 grams	FATS: 4 grams

½ cup blackberries

½ cup raspberries

½ cup blueberries

½ cup chopped mango

1 cup coarsely chopped kale

2 teaspoons elderberry syrup

1 cup almond milk

BETA-CARA-COOLER

CALORIES: 299	CARBS: 70 grams
PROTEINS: 7 grams	FATS: 0 grams

1 cup chopped cantaloupe

1 cup sweet potato*

1 cup spinach

½ grapefruit, peeled and seeded, or juiced

water and ice, to taste

Bake sweet potato in oven for about 1 hour at 350°F. Allow to cool in refrigerator overnight.

SWEET WINTER MORNING

CALORIES: 195	**CARBS:** 47 grams
PROTEINS: 4 grams	**FATS:** 0 grams

1 cup blueberries

1 banana

1 cup spinach

1 cup cold, unsweetened prepared green tea

GOOD DAY BERRY ELIXIR

CALORIES: 299	**CARBS:** 52 grams
PROTEINS: 7.5 grams	**FATS:** 11.5 grams

1 cup raspberries

1 cup blackberries

2 teaspoons peeled, minced fresh ginger

2 tablespoons ground flaxseed

1 cup almond milk

TANGY BOOSTER

CALORIES: 210	**CARBS:** 28 grams
PROTEINS: 4 grams	**FATS:** 10 grams

juice of 1 medium tangerine

1 kiwi, peeled

2 tablespoons chopped raw pecans

½ cup turnip greens

½ cup spinach

water, to taste

POM UP

CALORIES: 296	**CARBS:** 52 grams
PROTEINS: 5 grams	**FATS:** 12 grams

1 cup pomegranate juice

1 cup raspberries

1 cup spinach

2 tablespoons chopped raw walnuts

water, to taste

RHYMES WITH ORANGE

CALORIES: 222	**CARBS:** 54 grams
PROTEINS: 5 grams	**FATS:** 0 grams

1 medium orange, peeled

1 cup chopped cantaloupe

1 cup chopped carrot greens

1 tablespoon honey

1 cup coconut water

BOX OF BUDGIES

CALORIES: 222	**CARBS:** 56 grams
PROTEINS: 5 grams	**FATS:** 0 grams

1 kiwi, peeled

1 cup hulled strawberries

1 cup chopped mangoes

½ cup coarsely chopped kale

½ cup spinach

water, to taste

PAPAYA SOOTHER

CALORIES: 276	CARBS: 68 grams
PROTEINS: 6 grams	FATS: 0 grams

1 small papaya, peeled and seeded

½ cup chopped pineapple

½ cup hulled strawberries

1 banana

½ cup spinach

1 cup coconut water

EARTHLY DELIGHTS

CALORIES: 199	CARBS: 46 grams
PROTEINS: 5 grams	FATS: 0 grams

1 cup chopped carrots

½ cup sweet potato*

1 cup hulled strawberries

1 cup beet greens

water, to taste

Bake sweet potato in oven for about 1 hour at 350°F. Allow to cool in refrigerator overnight.

TURN UP THE TURNIP

CALORIES: 156	CARBS: 32 grams
PROTEINS: 4 grams	FATS: 3 grams

½ cup chopped turnip

1 cup hulled strawberries

1 pear, cored and chopped

½ cup turnip greens

½ cup spinach

1 cup almond milk

STRAWBERRY COCOA

CALORIES: 466	CARBS: 73 grams
PROTEINS: 13 grams	FATS: 15 grams

1 banana

1 cup hulled strawberries

½ cup cooked black beans, cooled

1 ounce dark chocolate

1 cup almond milk

FRESH C FOOD

CALORIES: 211	CARBS: 52 grams
PROTEINS: 5 grams	FATS: 0 grams

½ grapefruit, peeled

1 kiwi, peeled

1 cup chopped pineapple

1 celery stalk

1 cup coarsely chopped kale

water, to taste

EDEN'S ORCHARD

CALORIES: 284	CARBS: 72 grams
PROTEINS: 4 grams	FATS: 0 grams

1 small apple

½ grapefruit, peeled

1 tangerine, peeled

½ small papaya, peeled and seeded

½ cup chopped mango

1 cup spinach

water, to taste

MEAN AND GREEN

CALORIES: 185	CARBS: 44 grams
PROTEINS: 5 grams	FATS: 0 grams

1 medium apple

1 kiwi, peeled

1 cup coarsely chopped kale

½ cup turnip greens

1 cup spinach

water, to taste

TWENTY

SMOOTHIES FOR THE LONG RUN

It's no secret that a healthy diet full of fruits and vegetables can improve your physical health, but did you know that certain foods can improve your focus, mental energy and memory? In fact, certain antioxidants, vitamins, nutrients and even stimulants like caffeine can help prevent age-related memory problems like Alzheimer's and dementia. Blackberries, blueberries, apples, chocolate, coffee, spinach, cinnamon, turmeric, pumpkin seeds and even broccoli are a few of the smoothie ingredients that have been linked to improved cognitive functioning.

This chapter also features recipes to help improve vision and prevent issues with eyesight you might face down the line.

MORANGO FRESCO

CALORIES: 199	**CARBS:** 28 grams
PROTEINS: 7 grams	**FATS:** 6.5 grams

1 ounce açaí puree or powder

½ cup hulled strawberries

½ cup blueberries

½ cup raspberries

¼ cup whole-milk Greek yogurt

1 cup almond milk

water, to taste

TWO CUPS OF BERRIES

CALORIES: 288	**CARBS:** 66 grams
PROTEINS: 6 grams	**FATS:** 2.5 grams

1 ounce açaí puree or powder

½ cup hulled strawberries

½ cup blueberries

½ cup raspberries

½ cup blackberries

1 banana

1 cup coarsely chopped kale

water and ice, to taste

PROTEIN AND ANTIOXIDANTS, UNITE!

CALORIES: 830	CARBS: 92 grams
PROTEINS: 21.5 grams	FATS: 46.5 grams

½ cup blueberries

2 bananas

¼ cup natural peanut butter

1 ounce dark chocolate

1 cup almond milk

water, to taste

ANTIOXIDANT INFUSER

CALORIES: 553	CARBS: 43 grams
PROTEINS: 11 grams	FATS: 41 grams

½ avocado, peeled and pitted

½ cup blueberries

½ cup blackberries

2 tablespoons flaxseed

small handful raw pecans

1 cup coconut water

LATE DATE

CALORIES: 266	**CARBS:** 61 grams
PROTEINS: 4 grams	**FATS:** 2.5 grams

1 cup cranberries

1 medium orange, peeled

1 banana

2 pitted dates

pinch of ground cinnamon

1 cup almond milk

SWEET BERRY ELIXIR

CALORIES: 391	**CARBS:** 52 grams
PROTEINS: 14.5 grams	**FATS:** 17.5 grams

1 ounce açaí puree or powder

½ cup blueberries

½ cup raspberries

½ cup blackberries

½ cup currants

1 cup spinach

¼ cup flaxseed

1 cup soy milk

APPLE OF MY EYE

CALORIES: 522	CARBS: 52.5 grams
PROTEINS: 9 grams	FATS: 34 grams

1 Red Delicious apple

½ avocado, peeled and pitted

1 celery stalk

½ cup boiled beets

1 lemon, peeled and seeded, or juiced

½ cup spinach

2 tablespoons flaxseed

1 tablespoon coconut oil

1 cup coconut water

water, to taste

CHOCOLATE AÇAÍ

CALORIES: 622	CARBS: 92 grams
PROTEINS: 18 grams	FATS: 19 grams

3 ounces açaí puree or powder

1 cup blueberries

1 banana

¼ cup cooked lentils, cooled

1 ounce dark chocolate

1 cup soy milk

water, to taste

TRIPLE A

CALORIES: 352	**CARBS:** 58 grams
PROTEINS: 5 grams	**FATS:** 11.5 grams

1 Red Delicious apple

¼ cup açaí puree or powder

⅛ cup blanched raw almonds

1 banana

1 cup almond milk

water, to taste

PUMPKIN LATTE SMOOTHIE.

CALORIES: 398	**CARBS:** 61 grams
PROTEINS: 7 grams	**FATS:** 17 grams

1 cup mashed pumpkin*

1 banana

1 tablespoon natural almond butter

pinch of ground cinnamon

pinch of ground nutmeg

pinch of ground turmeric

1 tablespoon honey

2 tablespoons coconut milk

½ cup almond milk

1 to 2 shots espresso, cooled

ice, to taste

* *Bake pumpkin in oven for about 1 hour at 350°F. Allow to cool in refrigerator overnight.*

AÇAÍ BREEZER

CALORIES: 245	CARBS: 42.5 grams
PROTEINS: 3.5 grams	FATS: 6.5 grams

3 ounces açaí puree or powder
½ cup raspberries
1 banana
½ cup dandelion greens
3 mint sprigs
1 cup almond milk
water and ice, to taste

THE TRIPLE B (BERRY BRAIN BOOSTER)

CALORIES: 581	CARBS: 100 grams
PROTEINS: 17.5 grams	FATS: 17 grams

½ cup blackberries
½ cup blueberries
½ banana
1 apple, cored and chopped
1 cup spinach
1 ounce bran flakes
¼ cup ground hemp seeds
1 tablespoon honey
1 cup almond milk
water and ice, to taste

DR. APPLE

CALORIES: 607	CARBS: 112 grams ·
PROTEINS: 16 grams	FATS: 13 grams

2 apples, cored and chopped

1 pear, cored and chopped

½ cup hulled strawberries

1 banana

½ cup spinach

½ cup coarsely chopped kale

3 ounces ground hemp seeds

1 cup coconut water

INTENSITEA

CALORIES: 418	CARBS: 74 grams
PROTEINS: 5 grams	FATS: 14 grams

1 apple

½ avocado, peeled and pitted

2 kiwis, peeled

1 cup spinach

1 cup prepared green tea, cooled

1 tablespoon honey

water and ice, to taste

VISION-BOOSTING SMOOTHIES

Having good vision is vital for everybody. Whether you are a competitive athlete looking to boost your on-court vision, a runner or cyclist hoping to avoid a dangerous misstep, or just somebody who enjoys that before-bedtime book, these smoothies are stuffed with beta-caratene, a B-vitamin that helps prevent cataracts and vision-related deterioration.

SWEET BEET

CALORIES: 268	**CARBS:** 49 grams
PROTEINS: 7 grams	**FATS:** 7 grams

1 cup chopped cantaloupe

½ cup mashed sweet potato*

1 cup beet greens

2 tablespoons coconut milk

1 cup coconut water

Bake sweet potato in oven for about 1 hour at 350°F. Allow to cool in refrigerator overnight.

MAIKA'I MAKA

CALORIES: 195	**CARBS:** 34 grams
PROTEINS: 8 grams	**FATS:** 4 grams

½ cup chopped mango

½ small papaya, peeled and seeded

1 cup spinach

1 cup soy milk

SIGHT FOR SORE EYES

CALORIES: 148	**CARBS:** 29 grams
PROTEINS: 4 grams	**FATS:** 2.5 grams

1 small papaya, peeled and seeded

1 cup chopped carrots

1 cup spinach

1 cup almond milk

water, to taste

THROUGH THE LOOKING GLASS

CALORIES: 209	**CARBS:** 50 grams
PROTEINS: 4.5 grams	**FATS:** 0 grams

1 cup chopped mango

½ cup sweet potato*

½ cup coarsely chopped collard greens

1 cup spinach

water, to taste

Bake sweet potato in oven for about 1 hour at 350°F. Allow to cool in refrigerator overnight.

SING SWEETLY

CALORIES: 210	**CARBS:** 50 grams
PROTEINS: 4.5 grams	**FATS:** 0 grams

½ cup chopped mango

½ small papaya, peeled and seeded

½ cup chopped cantaloupe

½ cup sweet potato*

1 cup spinach

water, to taste

Bake sweet potato in oven for about 1 hour at 350°F. Allow to cool in refrigerator overnight.

RECIPE INDEX

INDEX

FURTHER READING

Brazier, Brendan. *Thrive: The Vegan Nutrition Guide to Optimal Performance in Sports and Life*. Toronto, Canada: Penguin, 2007.

Boutenko, Victoria. *Green for Life: The Updated Classic on Green Smoothie Nutrition*. Raw Family Publishing, 2005.

Campbell, T. Collin. *The China Study: The Most Comprehensive Study of Nutrition Ever*. Dallas: Ben Bella, 2004.

Miles, Kristine. *The Green Smoothie Bible: 300 Delicious Recipes*. Berkeley, CA: Ulysses Press, 2012.

Pollan, Michael. *The Omnivore's Dilemma: A Natural History of Four Meals*. New York: Penguin, 2006.

ACKNOWLEDGMENTS

A special thank you to Alice Riegert, Kristine Miles, Matt Kadey and all the people at Ulysses Press for helping make this book happen.

ABOUT THE AUTHORS

Keith Sebastian is an author living in Huntington, New York. Originally from California, Keith brings an eclectic mix of West Coast and East Coast to his athletic pursuits: He practices yoga, surfs, runs, bikes and plays ice hockey. Keith began drinking daily green smoothies seven years ago and hasn't taken a day off from them since.

Samuel Barnes is pursuing his doctorate in clinical psychology in Berkeley, California. He believes that a healthy lifestyle, including a balanced diet and regular exercise, is a vital part of maintaining optimum mental health. Samuel plays recreational soccer, runs in the mountains and makes a smoothie every day. He has never made the same smoothie twice.